Monographic Journals of the Near East *Assur* 3/2 (November

PROVINCIAL GOVERNANCE IN MIDDLE ASSYRIA AND SOME NEW TEXTS FROM YALE

Peter Machinist
University of Arizona, Tucson

In the latter fourteenth and thirteenth centuries B.C., the Middle Assyrian state underwent a major expansion which raised it to the stature of a "great power" in the Near East. The efforts made to rule the newly acquired territories are the subject of this paper.

The first part is an edition of five previously unpublished Middle Assyrian documents from the Yale Babylonian Collection, which bear on the issue of provincial government. Although not an archive, all may be classified as economic and administrative (they include an agricultural loan and records of disbursement), all date apparently from the thirteenth century, and all come from the provincial site of Tell Amuda, or Kulišḫinaš as it seems to have been called in this period. The texts thus link up, at least in date and provenience, with several of those published by M.-J. Aynard, J.-M. Durand, and P. Amiet in *Assur* 3/1 (July, 1980).

With these texts as a point of departure, the paper goes on to collect the other evidence for the system of provincial governance in Middle Assyria during the fourteenth and thirteenth centuries. The stages of growth of that system are charted, and the nature of its various territorial units and the personnel who staffed them is analyzed in detail. The point is made that by the thirteenth century, at least, the provincial officials formed a clear class of royal dependents. Any effort to see in them testimony for an oligarchic control of the state by a small group of "great" families is unwarranted.

Table of Contents

I. Introduction*

Middle Assyrian studies have quickened decisively in the last decade and a half, with the excavations at Tell al-Rimah and several other previously unexplored sites, the resumed publication of texts from the main site of Assur, and a variety of analytic and synthetic studies on linguistic, onomastic, chronological, cultural, and socio-economic topics.[1] Yet compared with the Old and Neo-Assyrian periods, the published Middle Assyrian sources are still rather modest, and large uncertainties still remain both in basic facts like the number and sequence of the eponyms[2] as well as in subtler issues like the role of Babylonian culture in Middle Assyrian society.[3] Any new sources, even if they appear at first rather uninteresting, have something to contribute, the more so when they pertain to areas beyond the capital at Assur, from which the bulk of our evidence has come.

It is just such "provincial" evidence that this study will consider. The point of departure is a group of five Middle Assyrian economic and administrative texts from the Yale Babylonian Collection. They are published here with the kind permission of Professor W. W. Hallo, Curator of the Collection, and in copies made by the late Professor J. J. Finkelstein, who had graciously turned these over to me before his death. The copies have been collated and measurements of the tablets obtained with the help of Professor Gary Beckman and Ms. Ulla Kasten of the Collection, to whom my thanks are due. Further thanks go to Professors Hayim Tadnor and Norman Yoffee for their comments and suggestions.

The texts—clearly Middle Assyrian from their script, glyptic, onomasticon, grammar, lexicon, and content[4]—were purchased as a group by the Yale Babylonian Collection in 1957 from Mr. Fahmi Ilias Hashish of Amuda, Syria. There seems to be no reason to doubt the owner's statement that they were discovered locally, evidently at the ancient tell of Amuda,[5] all the more so because of the mention of the town *Ki-li-iš-ḫi-na-aš* in one of them (YBC 12860: 7; see below). But it is going too far to call them an archive, since nothing in their content specifically interconnects them. Now Tell Amuda and the adjacent modern town are located in the Ḫabur Valley about nineteen miles west of Nusaybin/Nisibis, on the railroad line that runs along the Syrian-Turkish border.[6] The texts thus come from a region well known as an object of Assyrian expansion; and how they may help us to understand this movement in the Middle Assyrian period will be examined in Part III of the present study.

*This study was completed while I was a Lady Davis Fellow at the Hebrew University of Jerusalem, and I should like to thank the Lady Davis Foundation for its generous support.

Abbreviations conform to W. von Soden (ed.), *Akkadisches Handwörterbuch* (Wiesbaden: Otto Harrassowitz, 1965) (= *AHw*) and/or R. Borger, *Handbuch der Keilschriftliteratur* I-III (Berlin: Walter de Gruyter & Co., 1967-75), with the following additions: Freydank-Saporetti, *Nuove* = H. Freydank and C. Saporetti, *Nuove Attestazioni dell' Onomastica medio-assira* (Incunabula Graeca LXXIV; Rome: Edizioni dell' Ateneo & Bizzarri, 1979). Saporetti, *Eponimi* = C. Saporetti, *Gli Eponimi medio-assiri* (BiMes, 9; Malibu: Undena Publications, 1979).

[1] A complete bibliography save for archaeological reports is given in Saporetti, *OMA* II, 358-75, updated in Freydank-Saporetti, *Nuove*, 225-28. The archaeology is surveyed, however briefly, in Walter Andrae, *Das wiedererstandene Assur*, 2.Auflage, ed. B. Hrouda (München: C. H. Beck, 1977); B. Hrouda, *Vorderasien I*, 207-13; A. Moortgat, *The Art of Ancient Mesopotamia* (New York: Phaidon, 1969), 105-25; S. Lloyd, *The Archaeology of Mesopotamia* (London: Thames and Hudson, 1978), 178-86; E. Strommenger, *The Art of Mesopotamia* (London: Thames and Hudson, 1964), 40-1, 434-37. For reports on individual sites, see R. S. Ellis, *Bibliography* (up to 1971) and the surveys appearing in *AfO*, *Iraq*, and *Sumer*.

[2] The most recent study is Saporetti, *Eponimi*.

[3] See P. Machinist, *CBQ* 38 (1976), 455-78, where further bibliography will be found.

II. The Amuda Texts

1) YBC 12860

(Plates I, IV; 6.5 x 5.5 cm.)

obv	1	5 ANŠE ŠE i+na ^{GIŠ}BÁN SUMUN	1	5 *emāru* of grain according to the old *sūtu* measure (and)
	2	5 GÁNA A.ŠÀ e-ṣa-du	2	5 *iku* of arable field,
	3	ša ^{I}Mu-KAR-^{d}AMA[R.U] TU	3	belonging to Mušēzib-Marduk,
	4	DUMU Re-ma-ni-DINGIR	4	son of Rēmanni-ilī,
	5	i+na UGU ^{Id}UTU-mu-KAR	5	loaned to Šamaš-mušēzib,
	6	DUMU Ib-lu-ṭí	6	son of Ibluṭu,
	7	ša ^{URU}Ki-li-iš-ḫi-na-⸢áš⸣	7	from Kilišḫinaš.
	8	il-qe SAG.DU ŠE	8	The principal of the grain
	9	i+na ad-ra-te	10	he will measure out
	10	i-ma-da-ad	9	at the end of harvest time.
	11	šum-ma ŠE i+na ad-ra-te	11-12	If he does not pay back the grain at the end of harvest time,
edge	12	la i-te-⸢din⸣		
	13	ŠE a-na MÁŠ i-lak	13	then the grain will (begin to) earn interest.
rev	14	šum-ma A.ŠÀ i+na tu-re-zi	14-15	If the field is not returned at the beginning of harvest time,
	15	ḫar-pi la i-ta-lak		
	16	bi-la-at A.ŠÀ	16	then the produce of the field,
	17	ŠE ù IN.NU	17	the grain, and the straw
	18	i-da-an	18	he will hand over.

	19	IGI Ib-lu-ṭu	19	Witness: Ibluṭu,
	20	DUMU A-di-KAR	20	son of Addi-(mu)šēzib.
	21	IGI Ra-⸢ši⸣-DINGIR	21	Witness: Rāši-ilī,
	22	DUMU Ṣil-lì-Ku-bi	22	son of Ṣilli-Kūbe.
	23	IGI Ba-ḫu-ú DUB.SAR	23	Witness: Baḫu'u, scribe,
	24	DUMU Ṣil-li-^{d}MAR.TU	24	son of Ṣilli-Amurru.
	25	ITI Ku-zal-lu U_4.15.KÁM	25	Month: Kuzallu; day: 15.
edge	26	li-mu ^{Id}AG-EN-PAB	26	Eponym: Nabû-bēla-uṣur.

[4] Middle Assyrian features in glyptic, onomasticon, and content are discussed in the following sections of the paper. As for the script, note such MA forms as ANŠE (e.g., YBC 12860:1; 12861:1; 12862:1); *da* (YBC 12860:18; 12862:6); *i+na* (ligature) (e.g., YBC 12860:5, 9; 12861:6); *ka* (YBC 12862:9, 18); *li* (e.g., YBC 12860:7; 12861:15; 12862:3; 12863:6); SAR (YBC 12860:23); *ta* (YBC 12860:15; 12862:14); and *tu* (e.g., YBC 12860:24; 12861:7; 12862:8).

Grammatical features include the MA declension of proper names (YBC 12860:6–see n. 7 below) and the Assyrian, though not exclusively MA, verbal forms *e-ṣa-du* (YBC 12860:2); *i-da-an* (YBC 12860:18); and *i-te-din* (YBC 12860:12).

Lexically, one may note the MA month names Kuzallu (YBC 12860:25; 12863:5) and Muḫur-ilāni (YBC 12861:14), as well as the general Assyrian, though again not exclusively MA, terms *emāru* (e.g., YBC 12860:1; 12861:1; 12862:1); and *līmu* (YBC 12860:26; 12861:15; 12863:6).

[5] This was reported to me orally by J. J. Finkelstein.

[6] Cf., e.g., Robert Boulanger, *The Middle East: Lebanon-Syria-Jordan-Iraq-Iran* (Hachette World Guides; Paris: Hachette, 1966), 482 + Map.

COMMENTARY

The text records a loan of seed grain and arable land to be repaid at harvest time—a type of transaction well known in the Middle Assyrian corpus from Assur. For one close parallel, cf. *KAJ* 62 (edited in Ebeling and David, *ARu*, 359-360: No. 62; most recent discussion in C. Saporetti, *Assur 14446; La Famiglia A* [Cybernetica Mesopotamica Data Sets: Cuneiform Texts 1; Malibu: Undena Publications, 1982], 30-31).

6, 19: *Ib-lu-ṭi/ṭu*. This name, recently attested in MA (Freydank-Saporetti, *Nuove*, 60), is an abbreviation of a name like DN-issû-ibluṭu "They called on DN and lived" (cf. ^{d}Nabû-alsīka-abluṭ in Stamm, *Nameng.*, 200). Doubtless the two occurrences on our tablet belong to the same person—the alternate *i/u* endings revealing the characteristic MA declension of personal names[7]—and he is thus both the father of the borrower and a witness to his son's loan transaction.

7: ^{URU}*Ki-li-iš-ḫi-na-áš*. This seems to be a unique spelling for a town otherwise attested as ^{URU}*Ku-liš-ḫi-na-áš*, which Weidner (*AfO* 10 [1935-36], 21:n. 148) discovered in documents of Ninurta-tukultī-Aššur and Tiglath-pileser I (twelfth-eleventh centuries).[8] In several of the Tiglath-pileser texts, Kulišḫinaš appears in a list of administrative districts of the empire, which are always given in the same order: Arba'il, Kilizu, Ḫalaḫḫu, Rimuššu, Idu, Katmuḫḫu, Šudu, Taidu, Amasaki, Kulišḫinaš, Aššur, *pāḫutu elītu, pāḫutu šaplītu*, etc. Weidner thought that no conclusion could be drawn from this order as to geographical location; but if we exempt the last three entries as placed for reasons of special emphasis and summary, then the list does in fact move geographically from east to west, across Assyria into the Ḫabur. Accordingly, Ku/ilišḫinaš would be in the area of Amasaki; and since the latter is in the Upper Ḫabur, probably around modern Nusaybin/Nisibis,[9] Ku/ilišḫinaš would dovetail nicely with modern Amuda not far away, whose tell seems to be the source of our present group of tablets. The result of this is that Ku/ilišḫinaš may just be the ancient name of the Amuda tell. And yet we must be cautious here, for while the tablet before us may have been found at Amuda and Ku/ilišḫinaš may be mentioned in it, nothing in the tablet signifies that Ku/ilišḫinaš was where it was written or deposited. We read only that Ku/ilišḫinaš is the residence of the borrower, suggesting that the creditor comes from somewhere else, undoubtedly near by. There is not even an indication whether the tablet is the borrower's or creditor's copy, which could have helped to resolve the issue.

One final observation may be made. In the twelfth-eleventh century texts of Ninurta-tukultī-Aššur and Tiglath-pileser, Ku/ilišḫinaš is described clearly as a provincial seat.[10] Quite possibly, therefore, it had already acquired that status in the time of our tablet, the thirteenth century, when, as we shall see, provincial centers are well attested elsewhere in the Habur region (cf. *ad* 26 and Part III below).

[7] See Saporetti, *OMA* II, 92f. and, with specific reference to a nominative after IGI as here in l. 19, E. A. Speiser, *Festschrift Koschaker*, 147.

[8] The association with Kulišḫinaš was called to my attention by J. J. Finkelstein.

[9] Cf. E. Ebeling, *RlA* I (1932), 93a.

[10] A list of tribute of the period applies the term *pa-ḫe-te*^{MEŠ} to Kulišḫinaš and other places (Weidner, *AfO* 10 [1935-36], 41-2, 21 and n. 148: No. 95:2 = V. Donbaz, *Ninurta-Tukulti-Aššur. Zamanina ait orta Asur idarî belgeleri* [TTKY VI/19, 1976], 15-6 and Pl. 1: A. 113:2).

14-18: Two different terms are envisaged for the loan of the seed grain and the lease of the arable field. The latter is to be returned at the time of *turēzu ḫarpu*, that is, when the grain of that field, having just reached maturity, has been cut down (see Landsberger, *JNES* 8 [1949], 291-93, 284-86; and, restated more clearly, A. Salonen, *AgrM*, 197, 210). At this point, the field has served its purpose, so to speak, and can go back to the creditor—unless the borrower wishes to keep it for another season, in which case he must hand over to the creditor as compensation the entire yield of the present season. As for the seed grain, the amount borrowed is not returned at *turēzu ḫarpu*, but later in the harvest at the time of *adrātu*. This is the moment, again as Landsberger has shown (*JNES* 8 [1949], 292; cf. the restatement in A. Salonen, *AgrM*, 197), when the grain, having been cut and threshed, is at last brought in and stored. Obviously, by requiring the return of his principal at this point, the creditor can be assured of getting a full amount of seed grain, uncontaminated with chaff as it would have been earlier in the harvest process.

26: This *līmu* dates to Tukultī-Ninurta I (1243-1207 B.C.).[11] according to the evidence in Saporetti, *Eponimi*, 119-20.

Seal impressions: Only traces of the two impressions remain, and they are of little independent value in confirming the dating by *līmu*. The better preserved is on the left edge. Here can be made out on the left side the large moulded head and part of the body and tail of an animal, probably a lion, with a bird of prey above it to the left. For a thirteenth-century MA parallel to this complex, cf. Porada, *Corpus* II, No. 603. On the right side of the seal, more faintly, is the body of another animal with a cat-like head. As to the second seal, impressed on the upper part of the obverse, all that can be discerned is its right side. Here are the sinuous body and feathered tail of what may be an ostrich or a griffin, perhaps in flight from a human or animal figure that may have originally existed to the left. For MA parallels with an ostrich, see a twelfth-century seal in Porada, *Corpus* II, No. 606E and, more relevant at least in provenience, several fragmentary thirteenth-century impressions from Tell Fakhariyah in the Upper Ḫabur (*OIP* 79, Pls. 70: VI and 77: 75-6 with p. 71; Pls. 71: XVI and 76: F 270 with p. 75). Examples of MA griffins are illustrated in Porada, *Corpus* II, No. 596E and 598E (thirteenth century), and 607E (twelfth century).

[11] This and succeeding absolute dates follow the chronology of J. A. Brinkman, *apud* A. L. Oppenheim, *Ancient Mesopotamia: Portrait of a Dead Civilization*, revised ed. with E. Reiner (Chicago: University of Chicago Press, 1977), 335ff.

2) YBC 12861
(Plates II, IV; 4.3 x 5.4 cm.)

obv.	1	ANŠE NIGIDA 1 BÁN ZÌ.DA^{MEŠ}	1	1 *emāru* 7 *sūtu* of flour
	2	ša ŠU ^{Id}IŠKUR-LUGAL-KUR	2	under the control of Adad-šar-māti,
	3	i-na UGU ^{I}ŠEŠ-SUM-na	3	loaned to Aḫa-iddina.
	4	[1 AN]ŠE NIGIDA 1 BÁN ZÌ.DA^{MEŠ} KASKAL	4	[1 *em*]*āru* 7 *sūtu* of flour for travel provisions,
	5	[i-na] UGU ^{I}Pu-ti-ni	5	loaned to Putini.
	6	[1 AN]ŠE NIGIDA 1 BÁN ZÌ-DA i+na UGU	6	[1 *em*]*āru* 7 *sūtu* of flour, loaned to
	7	^{Id}MAR.TU-SILIM	7	Amurru-salim.
	8	1 ANŠE NIGIDA 1 BÁN ZÌ-DA^{MEŠ} i+na UGU	8	1 *emāru* 7 *sūtu* of flour, loaned to
	9	^{Id}AMAR.UTU-l⸢e⸣-i	9	Marduk-le'i.
edge	10	1 ANŠE NIGIDA 1 BÁN ZÌ.DA	10	1 *emāru* 7 *sūtu* of flour,
rev.	11	i+⸢na⸣ U[G]U ^{Id}UTU-mu-K⸢AR⸣	11	loaned to Šamaš-mušēzib.
	12	2 ANŠE Z[Ì.D]A i+na U[GU]	12	2 *emāru* of f[lou]r, loaned to
	13	^{I}GIŠ.PI (=GEŠTU)-⸢^{d}I⸣ŠKUR	13	Ḫasis(?)-Adad.
edge	14	ITI Mu-ḫur-DINGIR^{MEŠ} U$_4$. 22.KÁM	14	Month: Muḫur-ilāni; day: 22.
	15	li-mu	15	Eponym:
	16	^{I}Q[í-b]i-^{d}A-š[ur]	16	Qibi-Aššur.

COMMENTARY

The text is a record of disbursements of flour in standard quotas–all, except the last, are for the same amount–to six workers. The disburser is perhaps an official of the provincial administration, as indicated by the *ša* ŠU (= *qāt*) preceding his name (1.2), rather than simply *ša* or *ištu*, which seem to be the rule in private contracts.[12] For what purpose the flour is intended is not clear: it could be for the workers themselves as food rations (cf. ZÌ.DA^{MEŠ} KASKAL in 1.4), or for the workers to manufacture into bread or beer malt that will be delivered elsewhere. Befitting the nature of the text as a simple bureaucratic memorandum is its inconsistency in writing *qēmū* (ZÌ.DA^{MEŠ} in l. 1, 4, 8; ZÌ.DA in l. 6, 10, 12) and in paragraphing (no dividing line, as expected, between 11 and 12).

1, 4, 6, 8, 10: *NIGIDA*. On this unit (=1 PI = *panū* = 6 *sūtu*), see Borger, *ABZ*, No. 480, 383; *AHw*, 822b, 2; Landsberger, *WO* 1 (1950), 373-76; and Postgate, *NRGD*, 79-80. Another MA example is to be found in *KAJ* 58 obv. 2.

[12] For a selection of MA examples, cf. Ebeling and David, *ARu*, e.g., Nos. 76 (*KAJ* 106) and 78 (*KAJ* 117).

[13] See ll. 20-1:
⸢li⸣-mu ^{I}Qí-bi-^{d}A-šur
[DU]M[U ^{I}]Ì. GÁL.DINGIR $^{\text{[LÚ]}}$A[GRIG]?
The text will be published by me elsewhere.

4: *ZÌ.DA*^{MEŠ} *KASKAL*. In *KAV* 119, a census of *ḫurādu* soldiers approximately contemporary (Šalmaneser I) with our tablet, the plural appears as ZÌD.KASKAL^{MEŠ} (l. 6). The Akkadian equivalent is probably *qēmū ṣidīti*, for which see ḪAR.ra = *ḫubullu* XXIII, V 6: [zì.ninda].kaskal = MIN.MIN (= *qé-me ṣi-di-tum*) (so *MSL* XI, 75; cf. Hartman and Oppenheim, *JAOS Spl.* 10, 28, 52: n. 96). Cf. also Proto-Diri 374f.: NINDA.KASKAL.[LA] = *ṣi-di-*[*tum*], *a-ka-al ḫar-*[*ra-nim*] (quoted in *CAD* A/I, 238b. s.v. *akalu*).

13: ^{I}*GIŠ.PI* (= *GEŠTU*)-^{d}*IŠKUR*. The difficulty with this name is its first element. GIŠ.PI would appear to be an abbreviation of GIŠ.TÚG.PI/GIŠ.PI.TÚG; and a possible Akkadian equivalent is *ḫassu*. The resulting name, Ḫasis-Adad "Adad is wise," is without a known MA parallel; but the use of *ḫassu* and *ḫāsīsu* as divine epithets is widespread (cf. *AHw*, 330b-331a; *CAD* Ḫ, 127, 128a). In addition, one may compare the related verb *ḫasāsu*, which does appear in personal names like Ilī-ḫasis "My god is mindful (of me)": (*CAD* Ḫ, 123a, [2]).

15-16: Two eponyms named Qibi-Aššur are listed by Saporetti, *Eponimi*, 55, 124-245. He dates the first, very tentatively, to Aššur-uballiṭ I in the fourteenth century; the second, more certainly, to the thirteenth century, in the second year of the reign of Tukultī-Ninurta I. If our tablet is to be related to the rest of the Amuda group, then it should belong with the later Qibi-Aššur, since the other dated Amuda texts all fall into the thirteenth century (YBC 12860: 26; 12863: 6-7; cf. also 12862: 15 *ad loc.* below).

In fact, there is a good chance that the earlier Qibi-Aššur is also of the thirteenth century, not the fourteenth, in which case either man could be the *līmu* here. This earlier eponym is the son of an Ibašši-ilī, and it is on the identification of the father with an eponym of Aššur-uballiṭ I that Saporetti ascribes the son to the same king. But this ascription does not necessarily follow. More likely, indeed, is that Qibi-Aššur the son was *līmu* under a later king. And an unpublished MA text from the Yale Babylonian Collection would seem to confirm the later dating. The text in question, YBC 6959, is an inventory of perfumes, dated to the disputed *līmu*.[13] The perfumes, it reports, belong to the daughter of Bēr-bēl-la'īte, who from the context should be a royal official in Assur.[14] This agrees with the fact that all the other occurrences of Bēr-bēl-la'īte in the MA onomasticon—nine of them—are of a *līmu* from Šalmaneser I (cf. Saporetti, *OMA* I, 176; Freydank-Saporetti, *Nuove*, 43). In short, we are dealing with the same Bēr-bel-la'īte in all cases. Now if this is so, it becomes difficult to push the date of YBC 6959 and thus the *līmu* Qibi-Aššur son of Ibašši-ilī back more than fifty years before Šalmaneser to Aššur-uballiṭ.[15] And a post-Aššur-uballiṭ date is just what we suspected for Qibi-Aššur on internal grounds. Where, then, should this *līmu* occur? Satisfying all the evidence the best, it may be proposed, is a date in the first quarter of the thirteenth-century—under Adad-nīrārī I or, at the latest, early Šalmaneser I—with the father Ibašši-ilī serving his *līmu*-ship toward the end of the reign of Aššur-uballiṭ I.

[14] See ll. 12-18:

ša DUMU.MÍ ^{d}*Be-er-*^{d}*EN-la-*⸢*i-te*⸣	(all the aforementioned items)—belonging to the daughter of Bēr-bēl-la'īte.
mi-im-ma an-ni-ú	All this which Aššur-iddin brought out of
ša ^{Id}A-šur-i-din ša iš-tu	the tribute destined for the king was de-
pi-qi-ti ⸢ša⸣ a-na LUGAL	posited in the Middle/Inner Palace.
ú-qar-ri-bu-ú-ni	
i+na É.GAL-lì ša qa-ab-li	
ša-ak-nu	

[15] Following Brinkman (n. 11), the reign of Aššur-uballiṭ ended in 1328 B.C., while that of Šalmaneser began in 1273 B.C.

Seal Impressions: Of the two impressions, on the left and right edges, only the latter is legible. Its remains appear to be a pursuit scene, with both figures facing left. The figure on the right is the human hero, his head covered with a conical turbaned crown and his left arm extended, perhaps holding a sword or similar weapon. To the left is the pursued animal: its long sinuous body, horns or crest at the head, and perhaps traces of wing all point to a griffin-like creature. Below it may be the edge of a star-rosette or sacred tree. All these features have parallels elsewhere in MA—cf., e.g., the griffins in Porada, *Corpus* II, No. 596E and 598E (thirteenth century) and griffin and human in combat, though facing each other, in *ibid.*, No. 607E (twelfth century)—but the parallels are not close enough to permit any precise dating of our impression on artistic grounds alone.

3) YBC 12862

(Plates II, IV; 5.7 x 4.2 cm.)

obv.	1	2 ANŠE 5 BÁN ŠE	1	2 *emāru* 5 *sūtu* of grain,
	2	^{Id}UTU-mu-š[e$^{??}$]-⸢l⸣i	2	(for) Šamaš-mušēli $^{(?)}$,
	3	DUMU ^{MÍd}IŠ$_8$.TÁR-le-at	3	son of Ištar-le'at.
	4	2 ANŠE 5 BÁN ŠE 2 e-ṣi-du	4	2 *emāru* 5 *sūtu* of grain (and) 2 harvesters,
	5	^{I}Ki-din-^{d}UTU	5	(for) Kidin-Šamaš,
	6	DUMU Ì.GÁL-DINGIR ḫu-ra-da-tu	6	son of Ibašši-ilī, the soldiers.
	7	2 ANŠE 5 BÁN 2 e-ṣi-du	7	2 *emāru* 5 *sūtu* (and) 2 harvesters.
	8	^{I}A-bat-tu	8	(for) Abattu,
	9	DUMU ŠEŠ-DU-ka	9	son of Aḫu-illika.
edge	10	2 ANŠE 5 BÁN 2 KI[MI]N	10	2 *emāru* 5 *sūtu* (and) 2 DITTO (=harvesters),
	11	^{Id}IŠKUR-šá-gi-me	11	(for) Adad-šāgime,
rev.	12	⸢DUMU⸣ ^{d}U.GUR$^{?}$-x⸢-x⸣ (-x)	12	son of Nergal$^{(?)}$-...
	13	2 ANŠE 5 BÁN KIMIN	13	2 *emāru* 5 *sūtu* (and) DITTO (=2 harvesters),
	14	^{I}[A]-⸤ta⸥-na-aḫ$^{!}$-^{d}UTU	14	(for) [Ā]tanaḫ-Šamaš,
	15	DUMU LUGAL-ki-i-DINGIR-ia	15	son of Šarru-kī-iliia.
	16	1 ANŠE 5 BÁN	16	1 *emāru* 5 *sūtu*,
	17	^{I}Ṣil-li-ia	17	(for) Ṣilliia,
	18	DUMU ŠEŠ-DU-ka	18	son of Aḫu-illika.
	19	2 ANŠE 5 BÁN 2 Ù	19	2 *emāru* 5 *sūtu* (and) 2 DITTO (=harvesters),
	20	^{I}Ur-du DUMU ^{d}A-šur-MU-PAB	20	(for) Urdu, son of Aššur-šuma-uṣur.
	21	1 ANŠE 5 BÁN ^{Id}UTU-ŠEŠ-SUM-na	21	1 *emāru* 5 *sūtu*, for Šamaš-aḫa-iddina,
	22	DUMU M⸢a⸣-nu-i-qip	22	son of Mannu-īqip.
edge	23	4 ANŠE 2 Ù	23	4 *emāru* (and) 2 DITTO (=harvesters),
	24	^{Id}MAR.TU-ia	24	(for) Amurriia.

COMMENTARY

This is a record, probably from the provincial administration, of disbursements of grain and harvesters to nine individual supervisors for the forthcoming agricultural season. Among these supervisors are a regular soldier (ll. 5-6) and evidently two brothers (ll. 8-9, 17-18). The tablet appears to be a provisional memorandum, as evidenced by the lack of a date, the laconic wording, the rather free and inconsistent use of ŠE (present in ll. 1, 4; absent in 7, 10, 13, 16, 19, 21, 23) and of the DITTO sign to stand for *ēṣidu* (sometimes preceded by the numeral 2: ll. 10, 19, 23; sometimes not: l. 13; and once not used at all where it might have been expected: l. 7).

6: *ḫu-ra-da-tu*. On this term, see Part III of the paper below. The plural form is surprising, and is probably to be understood with both Kidin-Šamaš and his father, Ibašši-ilī.

10, 13, 19, 23: *KIMIN/Ù*. In 10 and 13, the sign is the standard KIMIN logogram for DITTO. But possibly in 19 and certainly in 23, it is the rarer Ù. Though rare, this usage of Ù for KIMIN is understandable, given the similar form of the two signs and the fact that in NA orthography the reverse can occur: KIMIN substituting for Ù in the function of *u* "and" (von Soden-Röllig, *Akk. Syll.*^{3}, 52: No. 296a; Schramm, *EAK* II, 23 *ad* I 69). Another MA example of the usage appears in Köcher, *BAM* I, No. 18 and p. XV (noted by Borger, *ABZ*, No. 455).

11: *^{Id}IŠKUR-šá-gi-me*. This name is known once elsewhere in MA (Freydank-Saporetti, *Nuove*, 20) as well as in MB (Stamm, *Nameng.*, 225). Against these other occurrences, however, which have as their second element the expected verbal stative, *šagim*, our name has the unusual *šá-gi-me*. This should represent the G participle *šāgimu* (for *šāgimu* with Adad, see *AHw*, 1127b, 2); but why the oblique case is used is unclear.

15: *LUGAL-ki-i-DINGIR-ia*. This name, again unattested in MA (Saporetti, *OMA* I, Freydank-Saporetti, *Nuove*) though paralleled elsewhere (Stamm, *Nameng.*, 315; also 118, 210), touches on the important issue of MA royal ideology. To summarize it briefly,[16] one may note that until the thirteenth century certain restraints, deriving from the OA period, governed the language used to describe the status of the king vis-à-vis the gods: he was no god himself, simply "the governor of Enlil" (*šakin* ^{d}*Illil*), "the viceroy of Aššur" (*išši'ak/iššâk* ^{d}*Aššur*), or at most "the beloved" (*narāmu*) or "favorite" (*migru*) of a deity. In the thirteenth century, however, these restraints began to loosen under the impact of the new military successes and Babylonian influence. The monarch began to be talked about in more exalted, even divine terms, though in the end the inherited restraints prevented a complete identification of the king with the divine realm. Now our present name looks as if it belongs in this new environment, with its qualified assertion of the king's divinity. If so, we would have an indirect means of dating the tablet as a whole, which would agree with the thirteenth-century position of the other dated Amuda texts (cf. YBC 12860: 26; 12863: 6-7; and 12861: 15-16).

22: *Ma-nu-i-qip*. This name is attested in the NB and Seleucid periods (see *AHw*, 919a, s.v. *qiāpu(m)*, *qâpu* II, 2b), and may be found in MA also, if the form *Ma-nu-qi* = *Mannu-(i)qi-*

[16] Cf. the fuller discussions in A. K. Grayson, *UF* 3 (1971), 311-19; and Machinist, CBQ 38 (1976), 465-68.

<*ip*>, rather than = *Mannu-(u)qî* as Saporetti proposes (*OMA* I, 308; II, 135). In any case, the name pattern exemplified here, *mannu* + verb, is a familiar one in MA (Saporetti, *OMA* II, 135).

Seal Impression: The impression, again very fragmentarily preserved, is on the left edge of the tablet and proceeds in a leftward direction. Its right half pictures the rear part of a quadruped pointing into the earth, as though falling. To the left is the main figure, a warrior with his bow bent ready to shoot presumably at an animal which is now lost on the extreme left side (unless that animal be the one on the right half of the impression, suggesting that the seal was rolled with an improper balance of scene). Scenes of this kind are well known in MA glyptic, as evidenced, e.g., in A. Moortgat, *ZA* NF 13 (=47) (1942), 58-9: Abb. 11-18 (all thirteenth century); but once more the parallels are not exact.

4) YBC 12863

(Plate III; 2.6 x 4.1 cm.)

obv.	1	3 BÁN 5 SÌLA ma-al-ti-t[u]	1	3 *sūtu* 5 *qû* of drin[k], (from which were drawn)$^{(?)}$
	2	1 BÁN KAŠ a-na pa-ni	2	1 *sūtu* of beer for
	3	šub-re-[e]	3	Šubrû/the Subarian;
	4	5 SÌLA KAŠ a-na ^{I}⌈x$^{?}$]	4	5 *qû* of beer for ^{I}[PN]$^{(?)}$
rev.	5	ITI Ku-zal-lu U_4.⌈6.KAM⌉	5	Month: Kazallu; day: 6.
	6	li-mu	6	Eponym:
	7	^{Id}I$Š_8$.TÁR-KAM	7	Ištar-ēriš.

COMMENTARY

This is evidently a record of drink rations for certain individuals. The first line could be taken with the second as the rations for Šubrû/the Subarian named in line 3. But it is perhaps more sensible to understand it as the general amount of the items to be disbursed, which would account for the use of the non-specific rubric *maltītu*. Lines 2-5, then, would describe the specific rations to two individuals drawn from this general amount.

3: *šub-re-e*. This is an apocopated variant of the gentilic *šubarûm*, which seems to be peculiar to Hittite and Assyrian, especially MA, texts (see Gelb, *HaS*, 20-30). It may be a gentilic here or else a personal name, as is attested at Tell Billa = Šibaniba (Šubrī'u) and at Tell al-Rimah (Šubrī'a) (see Saporetti, *OMA* I, 466). If a personal name, it could, of course, belong to an Assyrian: note that the Šubrī'a in Rimah has both a father and sons with good MA names. But if the individual in question is a local, this would fit with the provenience of the tablet in the Amuda area, since Amuda was part of what the Middle Assyrians understood by Šubartu (Gelb, *HaS*, 45-46; Weidner, *IAK*, 58: n. 2).

6-7: Saporetti, *Eponimi*, 80-82, 89, identifies two and perhaps three eponyms named Ištar-ēriš, all of whom served in the reign of Šalmaneser I (1273-44 B.C.). Our figure, therefore, should be one of these, though which one is impossible to determine.

5) YBC 12864
(Plate III; 3.0 x 3.0 cm.)

obv.	1	[½]$^{?}$ SÌLA ⸢NIN⸣DA ra[-aṭ-bu$^{?}$]	1	[½]$^{(?)}$ *qû* of fr[esh] $^{(?)}$ bread.
	2	½ SÌLA ⌊sa⌋ bi[ ]	2	½ *qû* of . . .
	3	⸢½⸣! SÌLA ru kàt$^{?}$ [ ]	3	⸢½⸣ *qû* . . .
	4	1 NINDA me-dí-⸢ru⸣ [ ]	4	1 loaf of *mediru* bread . . .
	5	1 NINDA me-dí-ru ⸢x]	5	1 loaf of *mediru* bread . . .
edge	6	3 NINDA me-dí-r[u]	6	3 loaves of *medir*[*u*] bread . . .
rev.	7	2 BÁN$^{?}$ Ì$^{?}$ ^{Id}AMAR.U[TU-]	7	2 *sūtu*$^{(?)}$ of oil$^{(?)}$ (of) Marduk- . . .
	8	½ SÌLA ^{I}DI.KU$_5$-⸢x]	8	½ *qû* (of) Da''an- . . . .
	9	⸢½⸣ SÌLA ^{I}EN-LUG[AL/Š[EŠ-]	9	½ *qû* (of) Bēl-šar[ru-/aḫ[(ḫ)u-]
	10	[x NINDA] me-dí-r[u]	10	[x loaves] of *medir*[*u*] bread . . .
	11	[ ]^{I} A-bu-[ ]	11	of $^{(?)}$ Abu- . . .
edge	12	[ITI x] U$_4$.2⸢1$^{?}$.K] ÁM	12	[Month:]; day: 21$^{(?)}$.

COMMENTARY

This again seems to be a record of disbursements involving several individuals. In the present instance, the commodities are bread and perhaps oil (see *ad* 7 below), which conceivably are offerings to some sanctuary by the individuals mentioned. Note in this regard that all the other attestations of *mediru/midru* bread concern offerings (*AHw*, 651a; *CAD* M/II, 48a).

1, 2, 3, 8, 9: On the assumption that the amounts in 2, 3, 8, 9 refer to bread as in 1, this text describes bread both as weighed (1, 2, 3, 8, 9) and as counted (4, 5, 6, probably 10). Why the two quantifications are used here is unclear. One may note, however, that at least in NA texts bread loaves were regularly measured in ½ or 1 *qû* amounts (B. Landsberger and O. R. Gurney, *AfO* 18 [1957-58], 339e; cf. also 338-39 *ad* 148-73 on the subject of bread and flour, generally, in NA sources).

4, 5, 6, 10: *me-dí-ru*. This is a variant spelling of *midru*, a variant otherwise attested only in NA (*AHw*, 651a; *CAD* M/II, 48a). From the limited evidence, it cannot be determined what precisely *midru* means, though van Driel, *Cult*, 214, conjectures that it denotes the quality of the bread product.

7: 2 BÁN$^{?}$ Ì$^{?}$. This could also be read, of course, as the preposition *pa-ni*, perhaps with a preceding *a-na* restored at the end of line 6. But 2 BÁN Ì is perhaps better, because it would bring the present line into parallel with the following two, each of which has the pattern: amount in cubic measure + personal name. The appearance of oil, admittedly, disturbs the repeated mention of bread in the text, but it would begin to make sense, if the text, as suggested above, is intended to record various offerings to a sanctuary. Furthermore, while the measurement of oil in *sūtu* is unusual—I do not know of any other MA example—it is attested at least lexically (cf. A. Salonen, *HAM* II, 299i), and the subunit *qû* is found elsewhere, as in Nuzi, with oil (e.g., D. Cross, *AOS* 10, 15, noted under the corresponding Sumerian term *sila*).

III. Assyrian Provincial Administration in the Fourteenth-Thirteenth Centuries B.C.

Considered by themselves, the five Amuda texts we have been examining are unexceptional, even jejune. They are useful, however, insofar as they point to the larger question of how provincial administration worked in the Middle Assyrian state. That question, though touched on by previous scholars,[17] has never been treated systematically. We shall try to do so here, therefore, noting where our new texts contribute to the overall picture.

A. Sources for Provincial Activity

Our attention will be directed not to the Middle Assyrian period as a whole, but to the phase in which it first assumed great power status, and from which, as we have discovered, our Amuda texts come—the fourteenth-thirteenth centuries B.C. For this phase, admittedly, the information on provincial activity is meager and haphazardly distributed compared to what we know about the Assyrian heartland. But it is not wholly without substance, drawing as it does on (1) official "ideological" texts like royal building inscriptions and chronicles; (2) diplomatic and related international documents; (3) administrative documents from the heartland centers especially Assur and Kār-Tukultī-Ninurta; and (4) documents and other archaeological evidence from several provincial sites: Nippur in the *south*; Tell Billa = Šibaniba and Tell Bazmusian in the *northeast*; and Tell al-Rimah, Tell Šeḫ Ḥamad = Dūr-katlimmu, Tell Fakhariyah, and now our texts from Amuda in the *west*, the latter three specifically in the Habur Valley.[18] The Habur has thus yielded the most diverse

[17] E.g., J. J. Finkelstein, *JCS* 7 (1953), 116-17, 119-21, 124-25; P. Garelli, *Sem.* 17 (1967), 5-21; C. Saporetti, *ANL Rendiconti* XXV/7-12 (1970), 437-53; and for the twelfth century, E. F. Weidner, *AfO* 10 (1935-36), especially 14-5, 19-22, 24-7.

[18] The *official "ideological" texts* are collected now in A. K. Grayson, *ARI* I and *TCS* V with bibliography.

Diplomatic and related international documents include those from Amarna—*EA* 9, 15, 16—and from Boğazköy—especially H. Otten, *apud* E. F. Weidner, *ITn*, 64-8 and *idem*, *AfO* 19 (1959), 39-46.

The administrative documents from the heartland centers of Assur and *Kār-Tukultī-Ninurta* are scattered in many publications. The main collections are *KAJ*, *KAH*, *KAV*, and H. Freydank, *VS* XIX/NF III; and a full bibliography is given in Saporetti, *OMA* II, 262ff. and Freydank-Saporetti, *Nuove*, 225-28. As for *Nineveh*, since it has been much less explored in this period, it has yielded almost no administrative texts. A possible exception, depending on how one construes the date, is BM 123367: cf. A. R. Millard, *Iraq* 32 (1970), 173; J. N. Postgate, *Iraq* 35 (1973), 16-8; and Saporetti, *Eponimi*, 59, 83, 133-34.

Provincial evidence is to be found in: *Nippur*—J. A. Brinkman, *MSKH* I, 313, 315, 386, Pl. 7: No. 13. *Tell Billa = Šibaniba*—E. A. Speiser, *Festschrift Koschaker*, 141-50 and Finkelstein, *JCS* 7 (1953), 114-36, 148-69 (Bi 1-67). *Tell Bazmusian*—J. Laessøe, *Sumer* 15 (1959), 15-8. *Tell al-Rimah*—D. Oates, *Iraq* 27 (1965), 73-5, 76-7, 78-80; 28 (1966), 123-39; 29 (1967), 70-1, 74, 90-1; 30 (1968), 115-17, 133-35; 32 (1970), 2-3; 34 (1972), 85. The texts are published by H. W. F. Saggs, *Iraq* 30 (1968), 154-74

representation of any provincial area, and doubtless we shall have more from it as the current team sponsored by the "Tübinger Atlas des Vorderen Orients" pursues its survey and excavations there.[19]

B. Chronology and Pattern of Provincial Activity

Put together, these sources establish a definite chronology and pattern for Assyrian provincial activity during the fourteenth-thirteenth centuries. The beginning of that activity, they make clear, lies in the mid-fourteenth century, when Aššur-uballiṭ I (1363-28) took advantage of the Mittannian civil war and moved *west* into Mittannian territory in the Ḫabur and other parts of the Jazirah, even as he pushed *south* through the Lower Zab and Diyala Valleys into Babylonia, where he sought leverage by a diplomatic marriage.[20] In turn, his grandson, Arik-dēn-ili (1317-06), is credited with advances *north* and *northeast* into the the upper Tigris and Zagros.[21] All this, as is well known, represented a decisive break with the pre-Aššur-uballiṭ decades, which had seen the Middle Assyrian state subservient to Mittanni and Babylonia,[22] and confined to its Upper Tigris heartland.

Under the thirteenth-century monarchs Adad-nīrārī I (1305-1274), Šalmaneser I (1273-44), and Tukultī-Ninurta I (1243-07), expansionist activity continued along the three axes already laid out, though with deeper penetration *north* and *northeast* to the state of Ur(u)aṭri, *west* and *northwest* to the bend of the Euphrates near Carchemish and to the Na'iri lands, and *south* into the heart of Babylonia.[23] More important, the character of this expansion changed dramatically. In the fourteenth century we were dealing mostly with raids and indirect extensions of influence. The little evidence for Assyrian settlement beyond the heartland was concentrated on adjacent regions: thus, the one or two texts from

and D. J. Wiseman, *Iraq* 30 (1968), 175-205. *Tell Šēḫ Ḥamad = Dūr - katlimmu*–W. Röllig, *Or.* NS 47 (1978), 419-30; H. Kühne, *Akkadica* 10 (1978), 16-23; *idem*, *AfO* 25 (1974-77), 249-55; *idem*, AfO 26 (1978-79), 186-87. *Tell Fakhariyah*–C. W. McEwan, *et al.*, *OIP* 79; B. Hrouda, *ZA* 54/NF 20 (1961), especially 209-22. [For two newly revealed sites, Tell Fray and Šūri, and additional texts from Amuda, see n. 30 and the Postscriptum.]

19 See the preceding note s.v. Tell Šēḫ Ḥamad = Dur-katlimmu.

20 Weidner, *IAK*, XX:1, 31-2 = Grayson, *ARI* I, 58 § 384; Grayson, *TCS* V, 159:i 8′-17′ = Grayson, *ARI* I, 50 § 321-22; Grayson, *TCS* V, 171-72:i 5-14 = Grayson, *ARI* I, 50 § 324-25.

21 Grayson, *TCS* V, 185-87; Frag. 2 = Grayson, *ARI* I, 55-6 § 359-62; Weidner, *IAK*, XX: 1, 19-24 = Grayson, *ARI* I, 58 § 382.

22 For Babylonia, see *EA* 9: 31-5, and with it *EA* 15-6 = Grayson, *ARI* I, 47-8 § 307-18. For Mittanni, see E. F. Weidner, *PDK*, No. 2 obv. 6-9 and *HSS* 9: No. 1 = E. A. Speiser, *JAOS* 49 (1929), 269-75 and H. Lewy, *Or.* NS 11 (1942), 33-4. Cf. also such Nuzi texts as *HSS* 14:118 and 16:328, and the treatment of them–sometimes too imaginative in the connections it seeks–of H. Lewy, *Or.* NS 28 (1959), especially 5-15, 22-5.

23 See the official "ideological" texts concerning these kings as collected in Grayson, *ARI* I with references to the original publications, 57-8: No. 1; 60-1: Nos. 3-4; 76: No. 40; 77: No. 49; 78-9: Nos. 53*-54*; 79-83: No. 1; 87: No. 4; 92: No. 12; 93: No. 13; 101-4: No. 1; 105-6: No. 2; 106-7: Nos. 3-4; 107-8: No. 5; 109-10: No. 6; 110-11: No. 7; 112: No. 9; 112-13: No. 10; 114: No. 12; 115-16: No. 14; 117-19: No. 16; 120-21: No. 17; 123: No. 20; 124: No. 21; 124-25: Nos. 22-23; 126-27: No. 26; 127-28: No. 29; 133-34: Nos. 46*-7*. It may be added that Assyrian expansion in this period never really passed beyond the Euphrates bend because it was checked by the Hittites, who fortified Carchemish as their principal defensive installation. The tensions between the two powers over the area are reflected in a variety of diplomatic exchanges, especially those referred to in n. 18.

Aššur-uballiṭ I found at Tell al-Rimah west of Assur.[24] In the thirteenth century, however, we see a concerted effort at permanent control of provincial territory on a wide scale.

Our sources attest to this new situation in various ways. In the official "ideological" texts, we can trace the shift of emphasis away from periodic raids now to more durable solutions: first, to reducing an area to vassalage, with loyalty oaths, regular tribute, and often corvée service imposed upon the local ruler and his people; then, to converting the area to a province under direct Assyrian supervision. The paradigm here is the Ḫabur Valley and its ruling power, Mittanni/(or after the mid-fourteenth century) Ḫanigalbat, which, as the official texts record, passed from Assyrian vassal to province—or more exactly, a group of provinces—in the latter years of Adad-nīrārī I, and then was restored to provincial status, following a rebellion, by Šalmaneser I.[25] This general picture is confirmed by the other sources at our disposal. Thus, no provincial governors appear in administrative documents from the heartland centers of Assyria before the thirteenth century.[26] Likewise, of the provincial sites known, none, except for Tell al-Rimah mentioned earlier, has a pre-thirteenth century Middle Assyrian occupation.[27] This last point, it may be recalled, includes our Amuda texts as well, for where a date is indicated on them—so with varying certainty in four of the five (YBC 12860-12863)—it uniformly falls in the thirteenth century.

But we can be even more precise. If the move toward consolidation began only with the thirteenth century, there are various indications that it did not settle into place until the second quarter of the century, following the accession of Šalmaneser I. The first of these is

[24] See Wiseman, *Iraq* 30 (1968), 185: TR. 3037 and perhaps Saggs, *Iraq* 30 (1968), Pl. XLIV: TR. 2016 with the collation of J. N. Postgate, *OrAnt.* XIII (1974), 69. The dating is given in Saporetti, *Eponimi* 44 s.v. Abu-tāb and 47 s.v. Dān-Aššur. One other piece of evidence may also have to be considered, if Saporetti is right about placing the *līmu* Aššur-šēzibanni in the period of Aššur-uballiṭ I (*Eponimi*, 55). For the commemorative stela of this official describes him as *tartānu* and as *šaknu* of Nineveh, Katmuḫḫu, and Niḫria, indicating, thus, a fairly wide-ranging group of provinces in his lifetime. However, the proposed date of this *līmu* is at the very least uncertain, as Saporetti himself admits, and more likely should be lowered to the twelfth century B.C.: cf. H. A. Fine, *Studies in Middle Assyrian Chronology and Religion* (Cincinnati: Hebrew Union College Press, 1955), 93.

[25] See in Grayson, *ARI* I with reference to original publications, 58 § 381; 60-1 § 392-94, 398; 76 § 497; 77 § 511-12; 82-3 § 530-31.

[26] Cf. the lists of names of governors with reference to the texts which mention them in Saporetti, *OMA* II, 232-33, 244 and Freydank-Saporetti, *Nuove*, 199, 204 (s.v. *bel pāḫete*, *ḫassiḫlu*, *šaknu*). Dates of these texts are given in Fine (n. 24) and Saporetti, *Eponimi*. For a possible, though unlikely exception to the pattern, see n. 24 above.

[27] *Nippur*—Brinkman, *MSKH* I, 313, 315, 386, Pl. 7: No. 13 (Tukultī-Ninurta I).

Šibaniba—Finkelstein, *JCS* 7 (1953), 115; Saporetti, *Mesopotamia* VIII-IX (1973-74), 167-69, 176-79; *idem*, *Eponimi*, 4-5 and *passim* (Adad-nīrārī I-Tukultī-Ninurta I).

Tell Bazmusian—Laessøe, *Sumer* 15 (1959), 17-18. No dates are preserved, but as Laessøe notes, the surviving contents are not incompatible with the period of Tukultī-Ninurta I.

Tell al-Rimah—C. Wilcke, *ZA* 66 (1976), 229-33 and Saporetti, *Eponimi* 4-7. These two studies supersede earlier work by Saggs, *Iraq* 30 (1968), 155; Wiseman, *Iraq* 30 (1968), 175; and Saporetti, *Mesopotamia* VIII-IX (1973-74), 169-79, and provide dates in the reigns of Aššur-uballiṭ I (see n. 24) and then Šalmaneser I-Tukultī-Ninurta I. It is not impossible, however, that part of the "second generation" of the Rimah family of Atḫī-nādā could have been active also in the reign of Adad-nīrārī I.

Dūr-katlimmu—Röllig, *Or.* NS 47 (1978), 425; Kühne, *Akkadica* 10 (1978), 20-21; Saporetti, *Eponimi*, 176 and *passim* (Šalmaneser I-Tukultī-Ninurta I).

Tell Fakhariyah—McEwan, Kantor, and Güterbock, *OIP* 79:19, 23, 35, 42-45, 69, 85, 86-7; Saporetti, *Eponimi*, 182 and *passim* (Šalmaneser I-Tukultī-Ninurta I).

an official text of Adad-nīrārī I, which suggests that he did not live to complete the restoration of the capital of Ḫanigalbat, after he had ordained the transfer of the whole area to provincial status. That, evidently, Šalmaneser had to carry out.[28] Similarly, it is really only with Šalmaneser's reign that we begin to see the texts from the heartland centers mentioning provincial governors.[29] And finally, in all of the provincial sites yielding evidence, including, again, our Amuda corpus, the bulk of this evidence by far must be located in the period of Šalmaneser and afterward. Indeed, in only two sites, both closer and thus more susceptible than the others to the control of the Assyrian heartland, does the evidence begin earlier, and then just in limited quantity: Tell al-Rimah, which as we have seen opens with the reign of Aššur-uballiṭ I, and Šibaniba, which starts toward the end of Adad-nīrārī I's tenure.[30]

Of course, the process of consolidation we have been discussing did not affect uniformly all areas of thirteenth century expansion. Only states like Ḫanigalbat, which were perceived

[28] The text in question is E. F. Weidner, *AfO* 5 (1928-29), 92, 100 = Grayson, *ARI* I, 61 § 398, concerning Ta'idu, one of the capitals of Ḫanigalbat. As against another inscription of Adad-nīrārī, which describes the construction of a palace in Ta'idu with stelae (Weidner, *AfO* 5 [1928-29], 90-2, 97-9 = Grayson, *ARI* I, 61 § 395), this text has been left blank precisely where the building activities should have been recorded. It is possible that the text was a prototype for building inscriptions in Ta'idu (so Borger, *EAK* I, 40), but more likely is that the king died before the text and the building with which it was to be associated were completed (cf. Grayson, *ARI* I, 61: n. 122). Indeed, a later Assyrian monarch, Aššurnaṣirpal II, remembered only a Šalmaneser as the one who had "fortified Ta'idu" (*ú-šá-aṣ-bi-tú-ni* URU *Ti-i-du*: King, *AKA*, 239: 43-4 = Grayson, *ARI* II, 162 § 641); and it is tempting to suppose that the reference is to Adad-nīrārī's son, Šalmaneser I (so, e.g., K. Kessler, *Untersuchungen zur historischen Topographie Nordmesopotamiens nach keilschriftlichen Quellen des 1. Jahrtausends v. Chr* [RGTC, 1980], 95; Grayson, however, *ARI* II, 162 § 641, thinks that it is Šalmaneser II). In any case, several documents contemporary with Šalmaneser I show that Ta'idu was then functioning as an Assyrian provincial seat (*KAJ* 110, 121; cf. Saporetti, *ANL Rendiconti* XXV/7-12 [1970], especially 442-44, 450).

On the different fate of Ta'idu under the Middle Assyrians from the other major city of Ḫanigalbat, Irridu, see now Kessler, *RA* 74 (1980), 61-66.

[29] See nn. 24 and 26.

[30] See nn. 24 and 27. [A new site, much farther from the Assyrian heartland than Rimah and Šibaniba, may now have to be added, if we follow the recent publications of P. Matthiae and A. Archi, in *SMEA* XXII (1980), 35-51 + Tav. I-X, 31-2 + Tav. I-II. It is Tell Fray, located on the upper Euphrates about eighty-eight miles down river from Carchemish and twelve miles above the modern Tabqa (eth-Thawra) Dam, in whose waters it presently lies submerged. Here in 1973 a salvage excavation led by Matthiae recovered eleven Middle Assyrian tablets, described as "administrative and juridical" (p. 39) and said to date from the first part of the thirteenth century B.C. They were found in level IV, which otherwise showed a mixture of local Syrian, Hittite, and Mesopotamian influences; and Matthiae hypothesizes that they arrived there when Tell Fray and the Ḫanigalbat to which it belonged were converted into Assyrian provinces by Adad-nīrārī I. In turn, Hittite influence in IV, as exemplified by a bulla of Ḫattušili III and Puduḫepa, is placed especially after Adad-nīrārī, when Ḫattušili, presumably, aided Ḫanigalbat to throw off the Assyrian yoke and restore its native kingship, thus taking it under his protection. The final act was the destruction of level IV; and this, Matthiae suggests, occurred about 1265 B.C., as part of Šalmaneser I's reconquest of Ḫanigalbat and return of the region to provincial status.

The hypothesis just outlined is intriguing, but a full evaluation of it as well as of possible alternatives must await the final publications of the excavations. In particular, we still need a detailed analysis of the ceramic inventory of level IV, essential in fixing the range of its initial and terminal dates, and an edition of the Middle Assyrian tablets themselves (one is in press from G. Pettinato), by which the chronology and character of the Assyrian presence at Fray may be clarified. Doubtless even then, many questions will remain unanswered, for the excavations could operate only for one season and further work at the site is now impossible.]

as close enough and vital enough, economically and militarily, to the Assyrian heartland,[31] underwent the whole evolution from raiding through vassalage to province. Others, principally Ur(u)aṭri in the north, Uqumeni in the north/northeast, and the Na'iri lands in the northwest, hardly moved beyond the vassal stage, because they were too distant for direct control.[32]

Nor did the process always evolve smoothly and directly in the thirteenth century. Two regions in particular show modifications, reflecting the complicated problems of governance each posed to Assyria. The first was Ḫanigalbat itself, where in the course of the evolution already noted a special official appeared, charged with the overall supervision of the area. He was, as Borger first observed,[33] the *sukkallu rabû*, perhaps the highest Assyrian officer after the king; and the fact that as supervisor of Ḫanigalbat he carried the title *šar Ḫanigalbat* suggests that at least one intent of the whole effort was to preserve for the area a vassal-like status in order to counter the strong nativist sentiment within it. So understood, this post of "king" must have been created after–and as a deliberate variation on–the unsuccessful attempt by Adad-nīrārī I to govern Ḫanigalbat through a native vassal king. It would thus have overlapped the system of provinces established in place of the native vassal, though whether it began at the same time or only after the provinces were operating cannot be decided, because the first known *sukkallu rabû–šar Ḫanigalbat*, a certain Qibi-Aššur, could belong in the reign of Adad-nīrārī I, or Šalmaneser I, or Tukultī-Ninurta I.[34] Whatever the case, the provincial governors would have functioned under the authority of this Assyrian "king," who would have left them the bulk of the work, since as *sukkallu rabû* he resided doubtless in Assur, not in Ḫanigalbat. The situation, then, was not unlike that of the Neo-Assyrian period, particularly of the Sargonids, when major officials of the central

[31] The Ḫanigalbat region, it should be recalled, was important to Assyria in at least two respects: (1) it was a major breadbasket, especially in the Ḫabur Valley; (2) it lay athwart the major east-west and north-south trade routes to which Assyria needed access.

[32] On the vassal status of Ur(u)aṭri, Uqumeni, and Na'iri, see the descriptions respectively in Weidner, *IAK*, XXI:1, 2:2-6 = Grayson, *ARI* I, 81 § 527; Weidner, *ITn*, No. 1:III, 2-7 = Grayson, *ARI* I, 103 § 689; and Weidner, *ITn*, No. 16:49-56 = Grayson, *ARI* I, 119 § 775. Note further that no provincial governors are attested for these regions in our thirteenth century sources. In fact, the northern boundary of the thirteenth century provincial system did not apparently extend beyond the Tigris River as it flows around Diyarbakir and then east-west–Tušḫan and Bīt Zamāni being, perhaps, the northernmost provinces (cf. Kessler, *Untersuchungen* [n. 28], 85-121).

[33] EAK I, 21, 99, refuting there the thesis of J. Lewy, which more recently was revived and elaborated by E. F. Weidner, *Ugaritica* VI (1969), 526-28. Cf. also C. Saporetti, *Assur* 1/2 (June, 1974), 2-3 *ad* Stele 129 and *Eponimi*, 131-32. The point at issue concerns three officials (see below) who are described in inscriptions from the *Stelenreihen* found in Assur as PN SUKKAL GAL MAN ^{KUR}*Ḫa-ni-gal-bat*. Borger, followed by Saporetti, argues that this sequence must be understood as "PN, *sukkallu rabû* and *šar Ḫanigalbat*," not with Lewy and Weidner as "PN, the *sukkallu rabû* of the *šar Ḫanigalbat*." Indeed, one may add, if the latter sense had been intended, one might have expected a *ša* between *sukkallu rabû* and *šar Ḫanigalbat*.

[34] The problem here is that this Qibi-Aššur can be identified with either of two Qibi-Aššur's known as *līmus* in the Middle Assyrian period: Qibi-Aššur son of Ibašši-ilī, who, as suggested earlier (p. 7), functioned under Adad-nīrārī I or early Šalmaneser I; or Qibi-Aššur son of Šamaš-aḫa-iddina, whose eponymate came in the second year of Tukultī-Ninurta I (p. 7 above). How to decide between these is not clear. Our Qibi-Aššur is mentioned on one of the *Stelenreihen* (No. 63: Andrae, *WVDOG* 24, 61 and Tf. XXI:3, and Saporetti, *Eponimi*, 131), apparently as the first of a genealogy that stretches on through three more generations: Aššur-dammeq, Aššur-zēra-iddina, and Aššur-mudammeq. It is not unlikely, as has been noted

administration were also responsible for a province or provinces, the latter again managed by local governors.[35]

The dual posting of *sukkallu rabû* and *šar Ḫanigalbat* must have proved an attractive policy, for it turns up once more in our sources at the end of the thirteenth/beginning of the twelfth centuries, attached to the Assyrian Ilī-ḫadda, and may appear yet a third time in the Middle Assyrian period, though the latter instance is less sure.[36] More significantly, it cannot be divorced from what the Assyrians did to the other region of their expansion that offered them special difficulties, Babylonia. Here the path ran straight from raiding to province, bypassing the use of a native vassal king altogether. Yet the province established, at the direction of Tukultī-Ninurta I, bore a striking similarity to the arrangements made in Ḫanigalbat. For in Babylonia too, we read both of local Assyrian governors and of the assumption of the native crown by the Assyrian conquerors. The major difference, echoing the unique challenge Babylonia posed on the cultural as well as the political and military levels, was that the new Babylonian "king" was not the *sukkallu rabû*, but the Assyrian monarch himself, Tukultī-Ninurta–a practice that would later be imitated in Neo-Assyrian times.[37]

In sum, then, the thirteenth century Assyrian kings followed no simple path in their governance of outside territories. Yet clearly emerging from the variety of approaches is an aggressive policy of territorial expansion and consolidation well beyond what their fourteenth century predecessors had essayed. That this policy was a conscious one is underscored by the titles they claimed for themselves in their official texts. The most fulsome examples belong to Tukultī-Ninurta, reflecting the flowering of the policy in his reign. Here the climactic event was the conquest of Babylonia and assumption of the Babylonian throne–the first time an Assyrian monarch claimed the kingship of another state. Significantly, in the inscriptions composed after this event, the title "king" was generalized to the earlier conquests as well, so that Tukultī-Ninurta came to stand not only as *šar māt*

by Borger, *EAK* I, 21 and Saporetti, *Assur* 1/2 (June, 1974), 7 *ad* Stele 63 and *Eponimi*, 131, that Aššur-zēra-iddina, the third figure in this genealogy, is to be equated with a *līmu* known from the latter half of Tukultī-Ninurta I's reign, sometime after the conquest of Babylonia *ca.* 1225 B.C. (following Brinkman's chronology for Kaštiliaš IV, the captured Babylonian king: see n. 11). If so, his grandfather, our Qibi-Aššur, could fit with the *līmu* of Adad-nīrārī or Šalmaneser, because this would yield a comfortable time span–some fifty to sixty years–within which Aššur-zēra-iddina could have risen to his own prominence as *līmu*. On the other hand, it is not out of the question to identify Qibi-Aššur with the *līmu* of Tukultī-Ninurta's second year (=1243 B.C.), which would leave a span of at least seventeen years before the *līmu* of Aššur-zēra-iddina. Admittedly, this crowds the time; but the span could be lengthened if Aššur-zēra-iddina were understood to have held his *līmu* somewhat after the fall of Kaštiliaš in 1225, as appears possible (cf. Saporetti's implicit recognition of the problem in *Assur* 1/2 [June, 1974], 7 and *Eponimi*, 131).

[35] See the summary in P. Garelli and V. Nikiprowetzky, *Le Proche-Orient asiatique: les empires mésopotamiens, Israël* (Nouvelle Clio 2 *bis*; Paris: Presses Universitaires de France, 1974), 134-35.

[36] On Ilī-hadda, see Andrae, *WVDOG* 24, 85: No. 129; Borger, *EAK* I, 99; and Saporetti, *Assur* 1/2 (June, 1974), 2-3 ad Stele 129, and *Eponimi*, 132. The third example is uncertain because no personal name has been preserved on the stele in question: see Andrae, *WVDOG* 24, 87-88: No. 137a and Borger, *EAK* I, 21.

[37] For the Assyrian governors, see below p. 22 and n. 64. Tukultī-Ninurta's role as king of Babylonia is evidenced in two ways: (1) in his royal inscriptions he claims the traditional Babylonian royal titles (below and n. 38); and (2) in a recently discovered economic document from Nippur, the year date is given as ⌜MU⌝.SAG NAM.LUGAL.LA/TUKUL-*ti*-^{d}MAŠ "the accession year of Tukultī-Ninurta (=as king of Babylonia)" (Brinkman, *MSKH* I, 386, Pl. 7: No. 13).

Aššur, or even as *šar māt Karduniaš/māt Šumerî u Akkadî/*URU*Sippar u* URU*Bābili/māt Tilmun u māt Meluḫḫi*, but also as *šar māt Šubarî Qutî* and *šar kullat mātāt Na'iri*—indeed, finally, as *šar šarrāni*.[38] He had proclaimed himself, in short, as imperial sovereign.

C. Nature of Provincial Administration

Let us look more closely now at the system of provinces developed in the thirteenth century. As our sources admit, establishing such direct control regularly involved significant rearrangements of population, both to break the back of local resistance and to feed the growing appetite of the Assyrian heartland for a larger labor supply. The two most prominently documented instances are: (1) Babylonia in the *south*, whose conquest by Tukultī-Ninurta I brought numbers of Kassites north to Assyria, especially to Assur and Kār-Tukultī-Ninurta, where they seem to have been used in the extensive building projects then under way;[39] (2) the Jazirah, particularly the Ḫabur Valley, in the *west*, where, as Adad-nīrārī I tells us, his conversion of the native state of Ḫanigalbat to provincial status involved deporting the Ḫanigalbatian royal family and others to Assur.[40] His son, Šalmaneser I, followed this up with an even larger deportation: recorded in the latter's official texts is the removal of 14,000 "blinded" (*ú-né-pil* <*nuppulu*) Ḫanigalbatians, while various administrative texts from Assur in his reign show the reassignment of numbers of Ḫanigalbatians within the Ḫabur area itself.[41] Presumably, this increased population movement under Šalmaneser reflects his greater consolidation of provincial control noted above.[42]

To fill the vacuums created by deportation, groups were imported from elsewhere in the empire. The Ḫabur, for example, as Röllig has suggested, witnessed a transfer of people from Katmuḫḫu in the northest, at least one of whom became a governor of a province,

[38] For these titles and others using *šarru* which appear with Tukultī-Ninurta, see Seux, *ER*, 301-04, 307, 309, 318, and Grayson, *UF* 3 (1971), 311-17, the latter giving a view of the MA titulary as a whole. A similar piling up of titles with *šarru* recurs in the NA period, e.g., in the inscriptions of Esarhaddon (Borger, *Asarh.*, 80 § 53: 22-9).

[39] See Wiedner, *ITn*, No. 5/15:63-4 = Grayson, *ARI* I, 108 § 716: Weidner, *ITn*, No. 16:66 = Grayson, *ARI* I, 119 § 774; Weidner, *ITn*, No. 17:37-8 = Grayson, *ARI* I, 121 § 784; *KAJ* 103:12-16; *KAJ* 106: 10-14; Freydank, *VS* XIX/NF III:1, I 21'-22', 31'-32', 40'-45', IV 15-16, 22-3 (= Freydank, *AoF* I [1974], 58ff.); 71; VAT 18007 (unpublished; cf. H. Freydank in J. Herrmann–I. Sellnow [hrsg.], *Die Rolle der Volksmassen in der Geschichte der vorkapitalistischen Gesellschaftsformationen* [Veröffentlichungen des Zentralinstituts für Alte Geschichte und Archäologie . . . 7; Berlin; Akademie-Verlag, 1975], 60). For discussion, see Weidner, *AfO* 13 (1939-41), 121-23 and J. A. Brinkman, *RlA* V (1980), 470.

[40] Weidner, *AfO* 5 (1928-29), 90:48-52 = Grayson, *ARI* I, 61 § 393.

[41] The official text is Weidner, *IAK*, XXI:1, 2:33-35 - Grayson, *ARI* I, 82 § 530; the administrative documents include *KAJ* 109, 113, 121, 245. A discussion of the whole matter is given in Saporetti, *ANL Rendiconti* XXV/7-12 (1970), 437-453. Incidentally, it should be noted that *nuppulu* cannot mean "(fully) blinded" here, as already recognized by Borger, *EAK* I, 57 and W. von Soden, *Iraq* 25 (1963), 137, since with such mutilation the large number of captives would have been rendered virtually useless as laborers for the Assyrian state. Rather, the verb must refer to partial blinding in one eye or the like.

[42] In addition to those from Babylonia and Ḫanigalbat, other examples of deportation to the Assyrian capital area are known, particularly in the period of Tukultī-Ninurta I: (1) *Katmuḫḫu* (Freydank, *VS* XIX/NF III:27; for Katmuḫḫian deportees in the Ḫabur, see below); (2) *Na'iri* (Freydank, *VS* XIX/NF III:27); (3) *Bušše* (royal princes) (Freydank, *VS* XIX/NF III:1, I 49'-50' = Freydank, *AoF* I [1974], 60-61); (4) *Uqumeni* (Freydank, *VS* XIX/NF III:1, I 51'-52' = Freydank, *AoF* I [1974], 60-61); and, just

at Dūr-katlimmu.[43] And, of course, there were the Assyrians themselves: provincial officials, the army, merchants,[44] and others. Significantly, as is shown by the texts from the provincial states, including our Amuda group, these came not simply to administer, but often to settle, engaging in land and other transactions characteristic of the Assyrian heartland around Assur and Kār-Tukultī-Ninurta (see further below). And in such transactions especially, the natives and deportees seem to have played little or no part, for wherever we can check, the texts from the provincial sites reveal an overwhelming predominance of Assyrian names, that is, names that fit securely into the Akkadian-language patterns dominant in the texts from the heartland centers. At Amuda, for instance, they are all Assyrian, except for the name or epithet Šubrû, which, however, need not belong to a non-Assyrian (see list of names at end and commentary above *ad* YBC 12863:3). Our documentation, in short, appears to point to fairly self-contained Assyrian communities in the thirteenth-century provinces, governing but not integrated into the native or deportee populations.[45]

The provinces themselves of the thirteenth century—denoted by the Assyrian term *pāḫutu* (Babylonian *pīḫatu*) or, in at least one case, by the term *ḫalṣu*—were each centered on a particular city (*ālu*): hence the expression, particularly well attested for the Ḫabur Valley examples, *pāḫete ša*/*ḫalṣi* ^{URU}GN.[46] Around this center, in turn, were towns, villages, and manors with their associated fields, called (*āl*) *dunne* or sometimes, like the center, just *ālu*. The latter are best documented in the texts from Šibaniba,[47] but *āl dunne* turns up at least twice, once in connection with Tell Fakhariyah and once with Ta'idi of the

recently published, (5) the *Kašyari* region (H. Freydank, *AoF* VII [1980], 89-117). Not all these cases need imply that the areas affected became Assyrian provinces. Na'iri and Uqumeni, for example, seem to have remained in some kind of vassal status as noted above (n. 32); and it is possible, therefore, that (some of) their deportees were on temporary corvée-service in the Assyrian capital, not in permanent resettlement there.

For a general treatment of deportations in the MA period, see Freydank, in Herrmann & Sellnow (n. 39), 55-63.

[43] Röllig, *Or.* NS 47 (1978), 428-29.

[44] On merchants in Middle Assyria, see C. Saporetti, *SMEA* XVIII (1977), 93-101; *idem, Egitto e Vicino Oriente* III (1980), especially 183; and H. Freydank, *AoF* VI (1979), 269-71.

[45] The point here is clearly illustrated by the texts from Tell al-Rimah. While those from the thirteenth century MA occupation conform to the onomastic pattern discussed (cf. name list in Wiseman, *Iraq* 30 [1968], 187-95), the two tablets found in the preceding "Nuzi" level both show predominantly Hurrian names (Wiseman, *Iraq* 30 [1968], 186-87).

[46] *pāḫete ša* ^{UTU}GN is attested only as part of the title *bēl pāḫete ša* ^{UTU}GN, the occurrences of which are listed in n. 59. For *pāḫutu* alone as descriptive of a province, see *KAJ* 252:5; Freydank, *VS* XIX/NF III:71, 7; and perhaps Finkelstein, *JCS* 7 (1953), 135, 166 (Bi 61:3); 136, 168 (Bi 65:36).

Ḫalṣu is found in *ḫalṣi* ^{URU}*Bīt Zamāni* (Finkelstein, *JCS* 7 [1953], 124, 150 [Bi 6:8]). There is also an occurrence with ^{URU}Ekallātē (Finkelstein, *JCS* 7 [1953], 132, 162 [Bi 48:2]). But whereas the former instance appears to represent a province, as Finkelstein, *JCS* 7 (1953), 116-17 suggests, the latter seems of inferior rank, for it occurs as one of several areas whose troops are under the supervision of the *rāb ālāni* of Šibaniba province. *Ḫalṣu*, thus, would seem to describe territorial units of differing grades of importance, just like the related title *ḫalṣ*/*zuḫlu* discussed below (where further examples of non-province *ḫalṣu*'s are noted).

[47] Finkelstein, *JCS* 7 (1953), 128, 155 (Bi 20:15-16); 128, 156 (Bi 21:8; 23:7); 131, 160 (Bi 37:2); 132, 162 (Bi 47-50); 133, 163 (Bi 53, 54, 55?); 135, 167 (Bi 63:13).

Ḫabur region.[48] And in our Amuda texts, though none of these terms is mentioned, the pattern to which they refer can be assumed as well. Recall specifically text YBC 12860, where Kilišḫinaš, the home of the debtor, seems to be a provincial center, as it certainly was in the following twelfth-eleventh centuries, in which case the unnamed residence of the creditor could be an outlying *ālu*.

Now this arrangement of provincial center and surrounding *ālānu* was obviously modeled on the pattern at the imperial capital of Assur.[49] The modeling is also to be seen in various details. Thus, for Assur as for each provincial center—the explicit attestations are from Arbela, Ḫašuanu, Šibaniba, Tell al-Rimah, and the Ḫabur sites of Dūr-katlimmu, Amasaki, Naḫur, Šuduḫi, and Ta'idi—the nodal point was the *ekallu* (sometimes *ekallu ša* URUGN).[50] And where attested, as Garelli has pointed out, *ekallu* described both the physical complex in which the administration resided (= "the palace") and, by extension, the administration itself and its different functions (= "the Palace").[51]

Among these functions should be included: maintaining order in the province; overseeing agricultural production there—a task which involved the supervision of Assyrian and captive workers; and ensuring a regular supply of taxes in kind and, not occasionally, in personnel to the heartland centers, both palace and temple. Toward such ends, the provincial *ekallātu*, like their Assur model, served as repositories for grain, implements, and animals, as the sites of archives and weight standards.

The evidence for this range of functions is diverse. At Šibaniba, for example, the task of maintaining order is reflected in the proliferation of official lists of surrounding *ālānu* and personnel, several of which concern troop levies or the provisioning of troops.[52] The flow of taxes into Assur can be monitored on an inventory tablet discovered there and dating, probably, to the reign of Šalmaneser I, which records goats and *gukkallu*-sheep sent in by various northern and western provinces.[53] Conversely, the demand for taxes by the capital is apparent from a letter of the chancellor of Šalmaneser, Bābu-aḫa-iddina, which orders

[48] Tell Fakhariyah—Güterbock, in *OIP* 79:88, No. 2:4.

Ta'idi—*KAJ* 110:11-12.

Further, *ālu* alone in the sense of rural town or village seems to occur at Tell al-Rimah (e.g., Wiseman, *Iraq* 30 [1968], 180: TR. 3007, 13) and Tell Fakhariyah (Güterbock, in *OIP* 79:90, No. 11:7-8).

[49] See, e.g., I. M. Diakonoff in I. M. Diakonoff (ed.), *Ancient Mesopotamia* (Moscow: Nauka Publishing House, 1969), 204-34; and Garelli, *Sem.* 17 (1967), 5-21, especially 6-7.

[50] Arbela—*KAJ* 298:10-12.

Ḫašuanu—Finkelstein, *JCA* 7 (1953), 126, 153 (Bi 12:15).

Šibaniba—Finkelstein, *JCS* 7 (1953), 123, 150 (Bi 5:14); 125, 151 (Bi 7:4; 8:3); 127, 154 (Bi 18:2); 129, 157 (Bi 25:6; 27:12); 130, 158 (Bi 30:3).

Tell al-Rimah—Saggs, *Iraq* 30 (1968), 159: TR. 2021+2051, 4; 161: TR. 2031, 5; 165: TR. 2045, 3'; TR. 2048, 8'.

Dūr-katlimmu—Röllig, *Or.* NS 47 (1978), 426: No. 682.

Amasaki—*KAJ* 113:3-4, 11-12, 20.

Naḫur—*KAJ* 118:1-2; 120:17-18.

Šuduḫi—*KAJ* 109:3.

Ta'idi—Weidner, *AfO* 5 (1928-29), 90:55-60 = Grayson, *ARI* I, 61 § 394; *KAJ* 121:2.

[51] Garelli, *Sem.* 17 (1967), 6. Such usage, of course, was not restricted to the MA period; cf., e.g., the OB situation as discussed in N. Yoffee, *The Economic Role of the Crown in the Old Babylonian Period* (BiMes:5, 1977), especially chapter 1.

[52] Finkelstein, *JCS* 7 (1953), 131, 161 (Bi 41); 132-33, 162-63 (Bi 47-55).

[53] *KAJ* 314 = W. J. Martin, *Tribut und Tributleistungen bei den Assyrern* (StOr. 8/1, 1936), 21-3. For the date, see now Saporetti, *Eponimi*, 93 s.v. Bēr-bēl-līte.

the governor of Amasaki in the Ḫabur Valley to furnish cereal offerings to a temple.[54] How provincial governors would have responded to such orders may be illustrated by a text from Šibaniba which lists surrounding *ālānu* and the sheep collected from them, of which some, perhaps, would have been forwarded to Assur.[55] Finally, several kinds of documents attest to the role of the provincial *ekallu* in supervising agriculture. Most frequent are the ration lists and orders governing the distribution of grain: compare, for instance, the dossier *KAJ* 109, 113, 121, which treats the movement, through several Ḫabur provincial capitals, of grain rations for captive workers.[56] Additionally, we learn of the *ekallu* as agricultural storehouse in such texts as Bi 25 from Šibaniba, a receipt for a yoke lent by the *ekallu* to a worker, and No. 682 from Dūr-katlimmu, an order to distribute "grain from the grain of the *ekallu* of Dūr-katlimmu" to a certain individual.[57]

In the context of the preceding documents, it should be clear, the bulk of our Amuda texts find their place. The records of workers' rations (YBC 12861 and, apparently, 12863), one of which uses the official terminology *ša qāt* PN (YBC 12861: 2); the list of disbursements to agricultural supervisors for the forthcoming season (YBC 12862); and the inventory of what may be religious offerings (YBC 12864)–all indicate the presence of an active provincial administration, even if none of the texts explicitly mentions the *ekallu* or other official institution.

What now of the personnel who staffed and directed the provincial administration? Unfortunately, apart from one military title (see below), the Amuda texts offer no enlightenment. But our other sources do, and the major offices they reveal again show a derivation almost entirely from the pattern at Assur.

(1) The principal figure, of course–responsible for the functions of the *ekallu* described above–was the *governor*. He normally reported directly to the capital, where the extant documents show him in contact with various officials: in one case, already noted, it is with the royal chancellor (*sukkallu*); in another, with a royal attendant (*urad šarri*).[58] (For other connections, see below under [7] and [8].) Several designations are known for the governor, which may reflect geographical, chronological, or even functional differences, but the data are often too sparse to be sure. Of these the basic is *bēl pāḫete* (EN.NAM), attested, on present evidence, at a city which, if read Tal[mu]še, is north of Nineveh, and then otherwise only from the Ḫabur Valley: at Amasaki, Dūr-katlimmu, Naḫur, Šuduḫi,

[54] Freydank, *VS* XIX/NF III:39.

[55] Finkelstein, *JCS* 7 (1953), 132, 162 (Bi 47).

[56] Cf. the discussion in Saporetti, *ANL Rendiconti* XXV/7-12 (1970), 437-53.

[57] Šibaniba–Finkelstein, *JCS* 7 (1953), 129, 157.

Dūr-katlimmu–Röllig, *Or.* NS 47 (1978), 426.

On the palace as source of agricultural weight standards, see, e.g., *KAJ* 109:3; 113:2-3, 10-11, 19-20; 121:2; Finkelstein, *JCS* 7 (1953), 125, 151, (Bi 7:3-4; 8:2-3).

[58] Royal chancellor–Freydank, *VS* XIX/NF III:39.

Royal attendant–Finkelstein, *JCS* 7 (1953), 126, 152 (Bi 11). This text records the payment of a *šulmānu* to the attendant by the governor of Šibaniba, presumably for work done at the capital on behalf of Šibaniba.

and Ta'idi.[59] In addition, the title is known among the Assur officialdom as something like the supervisor of the Assur or Kār-Tukultī-Ninurta districts.[60]

A second designation is *šaknu* (or *šakin* GN), the essential equivalence of which to *bēl pāḫete* is supported by two twelfth century texts.[61] It too is used for officers in the central government,[62] but as a provincial title comes mainly from the twelfth century and later.[63] There are, however, at least four thirteenth century occurrences: one for Tusḫan north of the Ḫabur Valley; a second for what may be Apqu between the Ḫabur and the Tigris; the third for Babylonia under Tukultī-Ninurta I's occupation (though the source here is a post-thirteenth century Babylonian text, Chronicle P); and the fourth, at the end of the thirteenth century, for Katmuḫḫu.[64]

Finally, we must consider the title *ḫalṣ/zuḫlu*, a compound of Akkadian *ḫalṣu* and the Hurrian "vocational" suffix *-uḫlu*.[65] In the MA sources this appears once as *ḫalṣ/zuḫlu* and otherwise in two variants showing assimilation: *ḫassiḫlu* and *ḫa-siḫ*, the latter perhaps a construct of *ḫassiḫu* where the *-lu* has been omitted.[66] *Ḫalṣ/zuḫlu*s are attested as

[59] Tal[mu]še (or: Riše)–Saporetti, *Eponimi*, 118 s.v. Erīb-Marduk.
Amasaki–Freydank, *VS* XIX/NF III:39, 1-2.
Dūr-katlimmu–Röllig, *Or.* NS 47 (1978), 426: No. 685.
Naḫur–*KAJ* 109:10; 113:30.
Šuduḫi–*KAJ* 109:19.
Ta'idi–*KAJ* 121:4.

[60] Assur–*KAJ* 103:5; 106:4; 133:5; *KAV* 217:9.
Kār-Tukultī-Ninurta–Weidner, *ITn*, No. 35:3-4 = Grayson, *ARI* I, 130 § 841.

[61] The texts involve the official Eru-apla-uṣur. In the first, his commemorative stela in Assur, he is called *šakin māt Ḫalaḫḫi*; but in the second, the document *KAJ* 191:3-4, he is *bēl pāḫiti ša* ^{URU}*Ḫalaḫḫi* (cf. Saporetti, *Eponimi*, 134). One might wonder about the fact that *šaknu* is paired with Ḫalaḫḫu as *mātu*, while *bēl pāḫiti* joins Ḫalaḫḫu as *ālu*; but on balance this does not appear significant for a difference in rank, particularly because *šaknu* can be used with *ālu* (see n. 64 below s.v. Tušḫan and Apqu).

[62] Note *šakin Aššur* and *šakin māt* ^{URU}*Ninua* (Saporetti, *Eponimi*, 165, 131). Further, there is the title *šakin māti*, which appears to designate an officer of the central government, more particularly, according to the recent interpretation of Postgate, "the governor of Assur province" (*BiOr.* 37 [1980], 68; for examples, see Saporetti, *Eponimi*, 58 s.v. Aššur-šumu-lēšir; 129-30 s.v. Urad-kūbe).

[63] Cf. the attestations in *AHw*, 1141b, 2b, which, however, cover the *šaknu* both as provincial governor and as lower-ranked official. Further discussion, primarily of the NA data, is to be found in R. Henshaw, *JAOS* 87 (1967), 517-25 and 88 (1968), 461-83; and J. N. Postgate, *AnSt.* XXX (1980), especially 69-70.

[64] Tušḫan–Saporetti, *Eponimi*, 68 s.v. Ištar-idāja?.
Apqu?–Saporetti, *Eponimi*, 99, where the reading is given uncertainly as URU *Ap-q*[*a*?-*x*]. Kessler, *RA* 74 (1980), 66: n. 29, however, considers it to refer to Apqu.
Babylonia–Grayson, *TCS* V, 176:iv 6-7 = Grayson, *ARI* I, 134 § 873. Note that while this source suggests that Assyrian governors ruled in Babylonia, another late chronistic text, the Babylonian King List A, lists Babylonian native "kings" for the same period (Grayson, *RlA* VI [1980], 91:II 8-10). For various attempts to reconcile the discrepancy, see, e.g., H. Tadmor, *JNES* 17 (1958), 135-37; M. B. Rowton, *JNES* 19 (1960), 18-21; *idem. JNES* 25 (1966), 252-54; J. M. Munn-Rankin, *CAH*^{3} II/2 (1975), 287-90; and J. A. Brinkman, *PKB*, 65-7, 86-7. The problem has now been complicated by the discovery that Tukultī-Ninurta directly ruled as Babylonian sovereign, at least initially: see above n. 37.
Katmuḫḫu–Saporetti, *Eponimi*, 132 s.v. Mardukīja.

[65] See E. A. Speiser, *Introduction to Hurrian* (AASOR 20, 1941), 130 and F. W. Bush, *A Grammar of the Hurrian Language* (Ph.D., Brandeis University, 1964), 112-13.

[66] Or could it be in status absolutus? The issue is not apparently noted by Freydank-Saporetti, *Nuove*, 80, 92, 143, 148, who simply normalize it as *ḫassiḫlu*.

presiding officers over a variety of settlements. Some of the latter, echoing the etymology of our title, are labelled *ḫalṣu*; and in a recently published census of officials, they are found in undifferentiated, nameless groups, with the presiding *ḫalṣ/zuḫlu*s each described as ^{LÚ}*ḫa-síḫ rab* (GAL) *ḫal-ṣa-a-ni*.[67] Other settlements are "towns" (*ālu*) having specific names, Šibaniba and ^{URU}É.^{d}NIN (=Bīt Bēlti?); and here the officers are called ^{LÚ}*ḫassiḫlu* (*ša* ^{URU}GN).[68] Still another, from the same census as the *ḫalṣu* groups, is a "town" (*ālu*) of a specific population, the "Šantians," the title this time being ^{LÚ}*ḫa-síḫ rab* (GAL) *āl* (URU) *Šá-an-ti-ia-e*.[69] And lastly, there is a named "town" (*ālu*), Bīt Zamāni, located within a *ḫalṣu*, where the head is ^{LÚ}*ḫa-síḫ-li ša ḫal-ṣi* ^{URU}*Bit* (É) *Za-ma-ni*.[70]

Behind the various combinations just listed, as Finkelstein especially saw, is the notion of *ḫalṣ/zuḫlu* as chief of a *ḫalṣu*, i.e., as a military officer comanding a "garrison" or "district".[71] That notion is made explicit, in several of the newer examples not available to Finkelstein, by the connection with *rab ḫalṣāni*.[72] Yet we should not assume complete homogeneity here. For given that the evidence cited shows *ḫalṣ/zuḫlu*'s in various combinations, it seems likely that we are dealing with differing grades of that officer—more or less important in the provincial system depending on who each was and the nature of his settlement.[73] To specify all the grades involved is impossible in the present state of the evidence. But at least at two sites, Šibaniba and Bīt Zamāni, there is enough to argue—and again it is Finkelstein who has convincingly done so—that the *ḫalṣ/zuḫlu*s functioned as governors, equivalent to the *bēl pāḫete* and *šaknu*.[74] Not coincidentally perhaps, these two sites were related, in that the *ḫalṣ/zuḫlu* of Bīt Zamāni, Aššur-kašid, may also have held the title in Šibaniba, where in any case he was active and his son, Sin-apla-ēriš, was *ḫalṣ/zuḫlu*.[75]

One last point of significance: among the three titles for governor we have discussed, *ḫalṣ/zuḫlu* is the only one without parallel in the central administration in Assur or, for that matter, in the Babylonian bureaucracy. This is not an accident. Indeed, that the term was not native to Assyria is confirmed by its mixed Akkado-Hurrian etymology and the

[67] Freydank, *VS* XIX/NF III:5, 11-15.

[68] Šibaniba—Finkelstein, *JCS* 7 (1953), 126, 152 (Bi 11:4-5); 127, 154 (Bi 17:4-5); 129, 157 (Bi 25:3); 130, 158 (Bi 29:6); 130, 159 (Bi 31:3; 32:3).
^{URU}É.^{d}NIN—*KAJ* 224 = 296:15-16. The location of this *ālu* is unknown. [See now M.-J. Aynard and J.-M. Durand, *Assur* 3/1 (July, 1980), 47: n. 62.]

[69] Freydank, *VS* XIX/NF III:5, 16. Here ⸢LÚ⸣⸢*ḫ*⸣*a*-[*sí*]*ḫ* is restored from the surviving traces on the parallel of the preceding lines 11-15. This *ālu* cannot be located at present.

[70] Finkelstein, *JCS* 7 (1953), 124, 150 (Bi 6:7-8). The individual in question, Aššur-kašid, is also mentioned in other Šibaniba texts as *ḫassiḫlu* (Finkelstein, *JCS* 7 [1953], 127, 154 [Bi 16:5-6]; 128, 155 (Bi 20:5-7]) or, apparently, *ḫalṣ/zuḫlu* (Finkelstein, *JCS* 7 [1953], 128, 156 [Bi 21:5]). But it is not clear whether these cases involve the rulership of Bīt Zamāni or Šibaniba, since no place names are specified and Aššur-kašid may have ruled in both areas (Finkelstein, *JCS* 7 [1953], 117: n. 31; 127, 154 [Bi 17:4-5]).

[71] Finkelstein, *JCS* 7 (1953), 116: n. 30; 124.

[72] Note that in its other known occurrences—all in the NA and NB periods—*rab ḫalṣu* has precisely the function of military garrison/district commander. See *AHw*, 314a, 4 and *CAD* Ḫ, 52b.

[73] On the parallel situation with the associated term *ḫalṣu*, see n. 46 above.

[74] *JCS* 7 (1953), 116-17. Of particular interest is that in the NA period the Assyrian official over Šibaniba was called *šaknu*.

[75] See n. 70 above. If Aššur-kašid was *ḫassiḫlu* in Šibaniba, how this would have been coordinated with his rule in Bīt Zamāni and his son's rule in Šibaniba is not clear, as no precise chronology emerges from the Šibaniba texts.

fact that outside of Middle Assyria it occurs solely in Hurrian-affected areas of the later second millennium B.C., in all of which the form is the basic *ḫalṣ/zuḫlu* (or the slightly augmented *ḫalṣ/zuḫulu*), not the assimilated variants *ḫassiḫlu* or *ḫassiḫu.*[76] One may conclude, then, that the Middle Assyrian state adopted the term—and adapted it linguistically and otherwise—for its own developing provincial system from the local Hurrian environment, which it took over when it conquered Mittanni.

We turn now to several provincial officials subordinate to the governor:

(2) The *rab ekalli* was in charge of administering the physical complex of the palace and the personnel working within it. This is made clear in the texts concerning his activities as an official in Assur;[77] but it may also be presumed for the areas beyond, of which Arbela so far is the only attestation.[78]

(3) The *rab ālāni*, on the other hand, was the palace official responsible for coordinating the activities of the outlying *ālānu* with the provincial capital. He too is found at Assur;[79] but in the provinces of the thirteenth century, he has appeared so far only at Šibaniba, where, not coincidentally, the *ālānu* are best documented. His tasks, as the Šibaniba texts reveal, included arbitrating disputes in the *ālānu*, insuring that they received the necessary supplies from and delivered the required taxes to the provincial capital, and overseeing their participation in military and other work levees.[80]

(4) Within the *ālu*, the local supervising officer was the *ḫaziānu*, presently attested at Šibaniba and Tell al-Rimah, in addition to Assur and perhaps Nineveh.[81]

(5) Among what must have been a number of more minor palace bureaucrats should be mentioned the *alaḫḫinu* or "miller." Known in Šibaniba and a town URU[ ]-din-[ ] as well as in Assur,[82] he must not be imagined—at least not always—as a simple worker. Rather, as the *CAD* A/I, 296a correctly saw, he was an official responsible for the receipt of grain taxes from the surrounding *ālānu*, and then for processing and redistributing them,

[76] For these other occurrences, which include Nuzi, Alalaḫ (IV), and Amarna, see *AHw*, 314b, 1-2 and *CAD* Ḫ, 57. There the term did not necessarily have the range of functions it assumed in Middle Assyria, as is made clear by M. Maidman in his study of "The Office of *ḫalṣuḫlu* in the Nuzi Texts," *Studies on the Civilization of Nuzi and the Hurrians in Honor of E. R. Lacheman* (ed. M. A. Morrison and D. A. Owen) (Winona Lake: Eisenbrauns, 1981, 233-46.)

[77] Weidner, *IAK*, XX:6, rev 43 = Grayson, *ARI* I, 65 §425; E. F. Weidner, *AfO* 17 (1954-56), 268:6; 262f.

[78] *KAJ* 298:10-12.

[79] *KAJ* 107 = 117:2; 319:2 (Erīb-Sin).

KAJ 218:4; 263:4; 318:4 (Ubru).

[80] The texts concern the *rab ālāni* Aššur-šum-iddina, who appears sometimes with his title and sometimes without: Finkelstein, *JCS* 7 (1953), 136, 168 (Bi 66); 135, 167 (Bi 63); 135, 166 (Bi 61); 135, 167 (Bi 62); 136, 167 (Bi 64); 136, 168 (Bi 65); 132, 162 (Bi 48).

[81] Šibaniba—Finkelstein, *JCS* 7 (1953), 128, 156 (Bi 21:6-7).

Tell al-Rimah—Saggs, *Iraq* 30 (1968), 159: TR. 2020, 2′.

Assur—e.g., *KAJ* 103:1, 7; 106:6; 133:10; 215:27; 239:rev 4′.

Nineveh—A. R. Millard, *Iraq* 32 (1970), 176 and Pl. XXXVI: BM 123367 rev 1′. On the dating problem, see the references in n. 18 s.v. *Nineveh*.

[82] Šibaniba—Finkelstein, *JCS* 7 (1953), 125, 151, (Bi 7:6-7; 8:5); 127, 154 (Bi 15:9).

URU [ ]-din-[ ]-*KAJ* 263:7-10.

Assur—*KAJ* 318:5-6.

for example, to be used in festivals.[83] This supervisory role helps to explain the close association of the *alaḫḫinu* with the *rab ālāni* in various texts.[84]

(6) The numerous work batallions stationed in and around the *ālānu* had, naturally, their respective chiefs. So from Šibaniba, we read of a *rab ikkarāte* of the *ālu* Riša-[ ], who was to deliver a daily amount of straw collected by his workers.[85] Other *rab ikkarāte* appear in the area around Assur.[86]

Lastly, we note two officials whose work in different ways took them outside the direct authority and chain of command of a single provincial unit:

(7) One was the official discussed earlier, who combined the roles of *sukkallu rabû* and *šar Ḫanigalbat*.

(8) The other was the *qēpu ša šarri* or "royal agent." As the title indicates, the direct superior of this individual was the king, and so it is no surprise to find him well attested in Assur.[87] Provincially, he is known from Šibaniba, Tell al-Rimah, and various Ḫabur Valley capitals,[88] and his main task there seems to have been the supervision of inter-provincial transactions. The Ḫabur documents, for example, depict him facilitating the transfer of grain among Naḫur, Amasaki, Ta'idi, and Šuduḫi, in order to feed work gangs of captive deportees (*ṣābē nasḫūte*).

For the smooth functioning of this whole provincial apparatus, an essential, of course, was the army. The relationship here had various facets. On the one hand, the provinces furnished the army with an important source of recruits. Note in this regard a document from Šibaniba, which records a levy from the surrounding *ālānu*, carried out, evidently, by the governor on command of the Assur administration, for duty in a campaign against Ḫanigalbat.[89] On the other hand, the army acted to police the provinces and to provide to them personnel for agricultural and other work projects. Thus, we read in a text from Assur of the work details which an Assyrian general ([LÚ]*tartennu*) organized in the Ḫabur Valley for captive laborers, perhaps soon after Šalmaneser I's reconquest of Ḫanigalbat.[90] And from one of our Amuda texts (YBC 12862:4-6) comes the notice of an Assyrian soldier (*ḫurādu*) serving as a local agricultural supervisor.

How this army was organized and operated in the thirteenth century is not well known: a full study would have to consider evidence from other periods of Assyrian history and is out of place here. But several observations can be made about the major units involved and the terms for them, especially as these concern the provinces.

[83] Especially in Šibaniba (Finkelstein, *JCS* 7 [1953], 125, 151 [Bi 7; 8]).

[84] Cf. in *KAJ* 107 = 117; 263; 318.

[85] Finkelstein, *JCS* 7 (1953), 128, 156 (Bi 23). Cf. the related titles for battalions of different sizes: *rab* 5 *ṣābē* (Tell al-Rimah–Saggs, *Iraq* 30 [1968], 161: TR. 2030, 4) and *rab* 10 *ṣābē* (Šibaniba–Finkelstein, *JCS* 7 [1953], 133, 163 [Bi 51:14]).

[86] *KAJ* 91:5-6; 114:6-7.

[87] E.g., *KAJ* 113:33-34; 116:9-10.

[88] Šibaniba–Finkelstein, *JCS* 7 (1953), 124, 150 (Bi 6:14-15).
Tell al-Rimah–Saggs, *Iraq* 30 (1968), Pl. XLIII: TR. 2014, 13-14 as noted by Postgate, *OrAnt.* XIII (1974), 70 *ad* 381.
Amasaki, Naḫur, Šuduḫi, Ta'idi–*KAJ* 109:12-13; 113:7-8, 22-25, 33; 121:9-13.

[89] Finkelstein, *JCS* 7 (1953), 132, 162 (Bi 49; note also Bi 48).

[90] *KAJ* 245. On the date, see Saporetti, *Eponimi*, 99-100 s.v. Adad-bēl-gabbe, who hesitates between Šalmaneser I and Tukultī-Ninurta I.

Since the troops were, after all, only one of many classes of workers in the administration, they could be described–and not infrequently are, in capital and provincial texts–by the well-known general label for "worker," *ṣābu* (ERÍN).[91] Within such *ṣābū*, recent studies, particularly of Postgate and Freydank, have proposed to delimit three categories.[92] Two of these–*perru* and *kaṣru*–are of limited concern to us here, because up to now, they have appeared as contingents only in Kār-Tukultī-Ninurta, and because their military character is not clear. What is known about the *perru* indicates that they consisted of nonfighting professionals, whose connection, however, to the army proper remains to be worked out. For the *kaṣru*, no real descriptive detail is as yet available, though Postgate has conjectured, not implausibly on the basis of the related form *kiṣru/kiṣir šarrūti* in Neo-Assyrian, that they were a professional full-time corp of royal troops.[93]

Far more is known about the third category of soldier, the *ḫurādu*. In fact, this is the most frequently and widely distributed of the three, being the only one to occur in the provinces–so far, Tell al-Rimah, Niḫria, Katmuḫḫu, Šinamu, and now Amuda–as well as in the capital area–Assur and Kār-Tukultī-Ninurta.[94] The pervasiveness of this category is also underscored by the fact that it alone could be used more generally to denote "a garrison," "army," or "military campaign."[95] The nature of the *ḫurādu* has been clarified

[91] E.g. in Kār-Tukultī-Ninurta–Freydank, *VS* XIX/NF III:1 IV 33 = *idem, AoF* I (1974), 70-71–and in Šibaniba–Finkelstein, *JCS* 7 (1953), 131, 161 (Bi 41:2); 132, 162 (Bi 48:1, 9).

[92] H. Freydank, *AoF* IV (1976), especially 111-124; J. N. Postgate, *BSOAS* 34 (1971), especially 498-502; *idem*, in M. T. Larsen (ed.), *Power and Propaganda: A Symposium on Ancient Empires* (Mesopotamia 7; Copenhagen: Akademisk Førlag, 1979), especially 210-13.

[93] See the preceding note. The classic study of the NA *kiṣru* remains W. Manitius, *ZA* 24 (1910), 97-149, 185-224.

[94] Tell al-Rimah–Saggs, *Iraq* 30 (1968), 159 and Pl. XLV: TR. 2021 + 2051, 10-11, as corrected by Postgate, *BSOAS* 34 (1971), 499 and n. 14.

Niḫria–Wiseman, *Iraq* 30 (1968), 179 and Pl. LVIII: TR. 3005, 4-5, as corrected by Postgate, *BSOAS* 34 (1971), 498 and n. 9. The latter, 500: n. 19, locates Niḫria somewhere in the northern Ḫabur or Baliḫ Valleys.

Katmuḫḫu–Finkelstein, *JCS* 7 (1953), 126, 153 (Bi 12:17-18), as corrected by Postgate, *BSOAS* 34 (1971), 500 and n. 20. Note here that the *ḫurādu*'s are in a camp, apparently outside of the *ālānu* proper.

Šinamu–*KAV* 119:6-7, 10-11, with the notes of Postgate, *BSOAS* 34 (1971), 500 and nn. 17-18 and Kessler, *Untersuchungen* (n. 28), 81-2. The latter, 81-4, 110-20, discusses the location of Šinamu in the area just north of the Kašyari Mts.

Assur/Kār-Tukultī-Ninurta–passages collected by Freydank, *AoF* IV (1976), 111-13.

Two other MA occurrences may be mentioned. The first, unpublished, is referred to by *AHw*, 357 s.v. *ḫurādu* and lists three *ḫurādu* by their places of origin, which unfortunately are not specified in the *AHw* citation. The second, a letter to a Kassite king from one of his officials, dating to the first half of the thirteenth century, reports on various events in Assyria. Among them is the movement of *ḫurādu* of Ḫirana and Ḫasmu, the former of whom come to be stationed on and east of the upper and middle Euphrates (*māt Subarti, Suḫi, Mari*). It is not certain, however, that these *ḫurādu* are actually Assyrian troops in the process of being garrisoned, since at one point in the letter, unfortunately broken, they seem to be the object of pursuit by an Assyrian commander, Kī-pī-Aššur (O. R. Gurney, *Iraq* 11 [1949], 139 and Pl. XLVII:10, 4-6, 21-3; partial discussion by Kessler, *Untersuchungen* [n. 28], 82).

[95] Actually, from an etymological viewpoint, the use of *ḫurādu* in a more general way appears to have been original, from which the specific sense of a category of soldier was derived. Nonetheless, the point remains that only *ḫurādu*, not evidently *kiṣru* or *perru*, was used in such general *and* specific senses in the MA period. For *ḫurādu* elsewhere in the Near East in the late second millennium B.C., see *AHw*, 357b, *CAD* Ḫ, 244-45a, and, for Ugarit particularly, M. Heltzer, *OrAnt.* XVIII (1979), 245-53.

by Postgate, who argues persuasively that he was a non-professional draftee, called up for a fixed term of service from his home town[96]–thus, perhaps to be directly contrasted to the *kaṣru*.[97] Three pieces of evidence used by Postgate are worth our attention. First is TR. 2021 + 2051, a Tell al-Rimah record of a loan of a lance to a soldier while he is on campaign with the *ḫurādu*, which lance he is to give back when he returns home and so, presumably, is demobilized.[98] Second, there is a list from Assur, dated to Šalmaneser I (*KAV* 119), which notes various *ḫurādu* by their town of origin.[99] As this clearly echoes the military levy text from Šibaniba cited above, the latter text, though it uses the label *ṣābu usbutu* for the troops, may quite likely be referring by such to *ḫurādu*.[100] In other words, the recruits regularly demanded from the provinces may largely have been considered *ḫurādu*. Most important as an indication of non-professional status is TR. 3005 from Tell al-Rimah, which associates the *ḫurādu* with the *ilku*, the duty of periodic state service imposed on the citizenry.[101] In that text, it would appear, the *ilku* of the *ḫurādu* was fulfilled by campaign duty. But civilian work could also have been involved, as suggested by the presence of a *ḫurādu* as an agricultural supervisor in our Amuda text YBC 12862: 4-6. Indeed, it was doubtless the fact of *ḫurādu* service, whatever it entailed, that qualified as *ilku*.

D. Private Transactions in the Provinces

The activities of the Assyrian administration are not the only kind documented in the provinces of the thirteenth century. A variety of what look like private economic transactions also appear, paralleling those from the area in and around Assur. The most common type is the loan, with an optional clause specifying collateral. Usually, these are to finance agriculture and involve harvesters, arable land, and especially seed grain: so in the one clear private document from our Amuda corpus, YBC 12860.[102] But not occasionally in Tell al-Rimah and Šibaniba, they concern tin, which in Rimah can be in large quantities.[103] In addition, sales of land, wills, and records of the division of family inheritance by the heirs are attested.[104]

[96] *BSOAS* 34 (1971), 498, 499-501.

[97] Thus, especially in the large census list from Kār-Tukultī-Ninurta published by Freydank, *VS* XIX/NF III:5 = *idem, AoF* IV (1976), 113.

[98] Reference in n. 94.

[99] Reference in n. 94.

[100] Finkelstein, *JCS* 7 (1953, 132, 162 (Bi 49:10-11; cf. also Bi 48). On the term *usbutu*, see especially Garelli, *Sem.* 17 (1967), 13, who assigns it a meaning not incompatible with that of *ḫurādu* discussed here.

[101] Reference in n. 94.

[102] Other examples include:
Šibaniba–Finkelstein, *JCS* 7 (1953), e.g., 122, 148 (Bi 1); 123-24, 149-50 (Bi 3-5).
Tell al-Rimah–e.g., Saggs, *Iraq* 30 (1968), 173: TR. 2910; Wiseman, *Iraq* 30 (1968), 177: TR. 3001; 181: TR. 3013; 182: TR. 3015; 184: TR. 3022.

[103] Tell al-Rimah–e.g., Wiseman, *Iraq* 30 (1968), 178: TR. 3002; 181: TR. 3012; 182: TR. 3016; 185: TR. 3030, 3031.
Šibaniba–Finkelstein, *JCS* 7 (1953), 122-23, 148 (Bi 2); 125, 151 (Bi 9); 127-28, 155 (Bi 19). Cf. also the official list Bi 28 on 129-30, 158.

[104] Sales of land–Wiseman, *Iraq* 30 (1968), 179: Tr. 3004 (Tell al-Rimah).
Wills–Saggs, *Iraq* 30 (1968), 163-64: TR. 2037 (cf. re-editions by Wilcke, *ZA* 66 [1976], 224-29: Nr. 8 and J. N. Postgate, *Iraq* 41 [1979], 89-91) (Tell al-Rimah).
Records of division of inheritance–Güterbock, in *OIP* 79:89, No. 6 (cf. No. 5).

How these apparently private transactions should be related to the official public documents, like the census and ration lists, is not finally certain. But there are indications that the two groups should not be sharply separated. In the first place, the personnel involved in the private transactions can appear as officials in the public documents. The most explicit instance is the two governors (*ḫassiḫlu*) mentioned in the texts of Šibaniba, Aššur-kašid and his son Sin-apla-ēriš, who made and received loans in grain and tin,[105] even as they carried out such official responsibilities as overseeing grain deliveries for festivals[106] and the issuance of equipment for farm work.[107] Indeed, it is at times difficult to distinguish between the public and private activities of these two figures, especially in loan transactions. Finkelstein attempted to do so on the basis of certain formal criteria of the documents–presence or absence of witnesses, of the *ṭuppašu iḫappi* clause, and of official titles–but these are far from watertight.[108] The result is that we cannot always be sure, without further information on the status and objectives of the other parties involved, whether the loans in which Aššur-kašid and Sin-apla-ēriš were engaged were for their own estate or whether the provincial government, with them as representatives, was the active participant.

This interpretation of the public and private spheres is not so dramatically attested at other provincial sites, but there too hints of it can be found. Thus, at Tell al-Rimah, the only site so far published where we can adequately correlate types of texts and their findspots, both public and private documents seem to have been stored in the same structure–a temple, probably the major one of the site–with no marked segregation of one from the other.[109] The same may also be true at Tell Fakhariyah, assuming we can distinguish there public documents from the obviously private ones.[110] At that site, the structure is described as a large manor house, complete with a chapel and living quarters, including a paved toilet.[111]

Signficantly, in each of the three sites we have been examining, the documents, private as well as public, appear to revolve around single families. At Šibaniba, the power of that family is evident through its two members who were governors. At Rimah, though no such

[105] Finkelstein, *JCS* 7 (1953), 122-24, 148-50 (Bi 1, 2, 3, 5).

[106] Finkelstein, *JCS* 7 (1953), 125, 151 (Bi 7-8).

[107] Finkelstein, *JCS* 7 (1953), 129, 157 (Bi 25).

[108] Finkelstein, *JCS* 7 (1953), 120, where the suggestion is made that the public documents, as opposed to the private ones, (1) usually mention the governors with their official titles; (2) often lack witnesses; and (3) usually contain the *ṭuppašu iḫappi* clause. The very fact, however, that Finkelstein has to employ "usually" or "often" for these three criteria indicates that they are not reliable. Indeed, in a number of documents which Finkelstein classifies as public, the official titles are absent (JCS 7 [1953], 125ff., 151ff. [Bi 8, 9, 10, 13, 19, 26, 28, 30, 33]), while the witnesses are present (*JCS* 7 [1953], 125ff., 151ff. [Bi 9, 10, 11, 13, 14, 15, 16, 24, 25, 26, 30, 31, 34]). As for the *ṭuppašu iḫappi* clause, even P. Koschaker, on whom Finkelstein leans for much of the analysis, must admit that it appears in at least one otherwise private MA text in his corpus (*NKRA*, 143-44: n. 6, referring to *KAJ* 99). The whole matter is epitomized in a text like Šibaniba Bi 10. For Finkelstein this is a public document (*JCS* 7 [1953], 125-26); yet except for the presence of *ṭuppašu iḫappi*, its content is similar, say, to Bi 5, which Finkelstein makes private (*JCS* 7 [1953], 123-24), and it lacks the official titles but has the witnesses, which likewise, in Finkelstein's system, indicate a private text.

The problem of distinguishing public from private documents is, needless to say, not peculiar to Middle Assyria. Cf. for Old Babylonia, Yoffee (n. 51), 7-11 and *idem, JCS* 30 (1978), 30.

[109] See Oates, *Iraq* 29 (1967), 90-1.

[110] Here the items in question are texts 10 and 11 of Güterbock, in *OIP* 79:90, which look like official records of deliveries, but could possibly concern private manorial estates.

[111] C. W. McEwan *et al.*, in *OIP* 79, 19-20.

political status is attested, the family's importance can be seen through its far-ranging commerce in grain and tin, its ownership of estates in surrounding *ālānu*,[112] and most important, the fact that its archive(s) was mixed with public documents and deposited in perhaps the major temple of the city. The situation at Fakhariyah is least clear, because of the small and fragmentary lot of texts found; but here also we may suppose a family of influence from the manor-like house in which the texts were stored, which the excavator, not implausibly, has compared with the villas at Nuzi belonging to the wealthy aristocrats Šurki-Tešub and Šilwa-Tešub—the latter, incidentally, carrying the rank of *mār šarri*.[113]

Thus, the pattern in the Assyrian provinces of the thirteenth century begins to look like what we already know from the capital archives in Assur of the same period: large, extended families of wealth, holding estates and involved in a web of commercial relations, who have ties with, if they are not actually part, of the government.[114] Yet a final caveat is in order. The evidence discovered, both textual and uninscribed, is still too limited in numbers of sites and excavated areas within sites to say clearly that such families dominated provincial affairs. Even for those families we have examined, it is obvious that the available data do not allow a precise understanding of how they managed their interests vis-à-vis other private groups and the government.

E. Aristocratic Families Between Province and Capital

The probability, nonetheless, that aristocratic families existed at least somewhere in the provinces of the thirteenth century prompts the question: what were the connections, if any, to the similar groups known from Assur at the same time? To put the issue more directly, can we say that the families encountered in the provinces are but extensions of the great families of Assur? Postgate, for one, appears to think so. And in his view, the connections only confirm what he would conclude from other data at Assur: that in this period of Assyrian history the state as a whole "was in the hands of a number of 'houses' which . . . were run along commercial lines," in distinction from Neo-Assyria, where a "civil service" under royal direction did "much of the fiscal and administrative work.[115] Let us see, therefore, what connections can be established and whether they have the significance Postgate gives to them.

The evidence we must consider centers on a number of provincial officials of the thirteenth century, whose prominence in Assur was recognized by the receipt of a *līmu*-ship and/or other office:[116]

[112] Cf. Wiseman, *Iraq* 30 (1968), 177: TR. 3001, 3-5.

[113] McEwan *et al.*, in *OIP* 79, 18-20. Could the family have included those involved in texts nos. 5-6 (p. 89)? On Šilwa-Tešub, see recently M. Morrison, *JCS* 31 (1979), 3-29.

[114] Cf. Diakonoff (n. 49), 204-34; Garelli, *Sem.* 17 (1967), 5-21; and Postgate, *BSOAS* 34 (1971), especially 496-98.

[115] Postgate, in *Power and Propaganda* (n. 92), 202.

[116] This list excludes Uballissu-Marduk, a merchant whose activities Saporetti has documented in texts from Assur and probably Tell al-Rimah (*Egitto e Vicino Oriente* III [1980], 183). Being a merchant, however, Uballissu-Marduk cannot be shown to have established any real residence and therefore base of power in Tell al-Rimah; it was likely just a stop on his commercial excursions.

1)	Aššur-kašid	governor (*ḫassiḫlu*) of Bīt Zamāni and perhaps of Šibaniba	*līmu* under Šalmaneser I[117]
2)	Bēr-šumu-lēšir	*qēpu ša šarri* in Ḫabur, appearing in Amasaki, Dūr-katlimmu, and Naḫur	=? *līmu* under Tukultī-Ninurta I[118]
3)	Erīb-Marduk	governor (*bēl pāḫete*) of Riše (or Tal[mu]še)	*līmu* under Tukultī-Ninurta I[119]
4)	Ilī-ḫadda	*šar Ḫanigalbat*	*sukkallu rabû*; *līmu* under Aššur-nīrārī III[120]
5)	Ištar-idaịa	governor (*šaknu*) of Tušḫan	*līmu* somewhere under Adad-nīrārī I-Tukultī-Ninurta I[121]
6)	Kidin-Sin	governor (*bēl pāḫete*) of Šuduḫi	*līmu* under Šalmaneser I[122]
7)	Mardukīịa	governor (*šaknu*) of Katmuḫḫu	*līmu* under Aššur-nīrārī III, or later, in 12th century[123]
8)	Qibi-Aššur	*šar Ḫanigalbat*	*sukkallu rabû*; *līmu* somewhere under Adad-nīrārī I-Tukultī-Ninurta I[124]
9)	Urad-Šerūa	provincial agent in Ḫabur	=? *līmu* under Šalmaneser I or Tukultī-Ninurta I (see below)
10)	[.....]	governor (*šaknu*) of Apqu (?)	*tartānu*; *rab ekalli*; *abarakku rabû*; *līmu* under Šalmaneser I or before[125]

Now by itself the association of provincial officials with the *līmu* or other office in the central administration is only a starting point. It does not require the assumption that such officials belonged to the great families of Assur, much less prove that those families dominated the government. One could just as easily argue that these were ordinary civil service officials–a not implausible alternative, given that in Neo-Assyria, when Postgate supposes

[117] Cf. Saporetti, *Eponimi*, 75.
[118] Saporetti, *Eponimi*, 102-3.
[119] Saporetti, *Eponimi*, 118.
[120] Saporetti, *Eponimi*, 131-32. See discussion above on pp. 16-17.
[121] Saporetti, *Eponimi*, 68.
[122] Saporetti, *Eponimi*, 82.
[123] Saporetti, *Eponimi*, 132.
[124] On the problem of the date, see n. 34.
[125] Saporetti, *Eponimi*, 99. Cf. Kessler, *RA* 74 (1980), 66: n. 29.

the existence of a civil service, provincial officials were also regularly included among the *līmu* lists.[126]

To deal with our issues, therefore, we must ask if anything is known about the family connections of the provincial officials just listed. For five of them, there is indeed something. Unfortunately, two of these give us information that is one-sided. Thus, the pervasive influence of Aššur-kašid, his son Sin-apla-ēriš, and other relatives is well documented in the provincial area of Šibaniba, as we have seen; but no family connections in the capital at Assur are known. Conversely, Qibi-Aššur, if he is to be identified with the *līmu* Qibi-Aššur son of Šamaš-aḫa-iddina, is attested in the capital as a participant in various enterprises with his brothers Ištar-ēriš and Ubru, themselves prominent figures of the state.[127] But we cannot establish any family activities in the provinces, in fact no activity there even for Qibi-Aššur alone, which fits with the suggestion, made earlier, that in his role as *šar Ḫanigalbat* he operated primarily from Assur.

Similarly, the other named *šar Ḫanigalbat* on our list, Ilī-ḫadda, is not attested in the provinces himself. Yet his son is: a certain Mardukīia, who, as our list indicates, was governor of Katmuḫḫu perhaps around the turn of the twelfth century.[128] Assuming, then, that Ilī-ḫadda was based in Assur, we have here evidence for family connections between capital and province. The most extensively documented of such connections, however, belongs to one other official, Urad-Šerūa; and it is not surprising that he is the one Postgate appeals to for his views.[129] In Assur, the prominence of this official's family can already be recognized with his grandfather, Aššur-aḫa-iddina, a well established landowner there. It is again evident with Urad-Šerūa himself, who had a range of business ventures in Assur, and married into an Assur family of note. On the provincial side, the family's fortunes can be followed in the wake of Šalmaneser I's reconquest of Ḫanigalbat. Significant for the connections with the capital, the dossier on this provincial activity was deposited not in an archive in the Ḫabur, but in Assur. From it we learn about the appointment of Urad-Šerua's father, Melisaḫ, as governor (*bēl pāḫete*) of Naḫur, and also of Urad-Šerūa's own appointment, which overlapped in time that of Melisaḫ, as a provincial agent, working with several *qēpūtu ša šarri* and Melisaḫ in the distribution of grain. Later, perhaps, Urad-Šerūa turns up back in Assur, continuing his involvement in western affairs by arranging a transfer of captive Hurrian laborers from the capital to a *tartennu* in the Kašyari region. And we find him once more active in the west, at Tell al-Rimah, taking part in what may have been private transactions.

Thus, the cases of Urad-Šerūa, and of Mardukīia and Ilī-ḫadda do seem to reveal aristocratic families from Assur seeking to extend their influence outside, as a provincial administration developed in the thirteenth century. But the question remains: how representative are they? Can we assume that the same pattern applied to the other provincial officials listed

[126] See A. Ungnad, *RlA* II (1938), especially 412: n. 2; 429-32.

[127] On the problem of the identification, see n. 34. The activities of the three brothers are presented in H. Hirsch, *AfO* 23 (1970), 79-83. Add the textual corrections of H. Freydank, *OLZ* 66 (1971), 534-36 and his copy in *idem*, *VS* XIX/NF III: 6.

[128] Of course, if he actually belongs in the twelfth century, then, strictly speaking, he must be disqualified from our discussion of thirteenth-century developments.

[129] Postgate, in *Power and Propaganda* (n. 92), 202; 219: n. 16. For the family of Urad-Šerūa, see the following, where references to the relevant sources will be found: Weidner, *AfO* 13 (1939-41), 122; Fine (n. 24), 67-73; Saporetti, *ANL Rendiconti* XXV/7-12 (1970), especially 444-47; Garelli, *Sem.* 17 (1967), 16-18; K. Deller and C. Saporetti, *OrAnt.* 9 (1970), 57; and C. Saporetti, *SMEA* XI (1970), 149.

above, and so to the whole senior echelon of the provincial administration? Probably to some of these, yes; but that the great families of Assur were not always the source of such officials is suggested by the case of Katmuḫḫaia, governor (*bēl pāḫete*) of Dūr-katlimmu and, as his name indicates, a man whose native origins are best sought not in Assur, but in the subordinate region of Katmuḫḫu.[130] Furthermore, among the Assyrians attested in texts which have been found in provincial sites–including our Amuda tablets–almost none, aside from the *līmu*s, can be connected with individuals mentioned in texts from the capital area of Assur and Kār-Tukultī-Ninurta.[131] Admittedly, these provincial personages were mostly minor officials at best, and so one would not expect to be able to trace them easily at the capital. Yet if the great Assur families did really pervade and dominate the provincial administration, at least some of the personages should have been traceable, on the argument that as *clientelae* of the families, they followed them from Assur out to the provinces.

The role of the great Assur families in the provinces, then, must not be exaggerated: they certainly were involved, but the explicit evidence for this is small and is to be counterbalanced by other data pointing to other pattern(s). On these grounds alone, we may be suspicious of Postgate's view about the political dominance of the great families, at least as far as the provinces are concerned. And our suspicion is confirmed when we look more closely at the position of the king in provincial life. Four observations are in order: (1) Even the family of Urad-Šerūa, the main group we can document from capital to province, carried out their provincial business "on command of the king" (*ina abat šarri*).[132] (2) That this was not an empty phrase is made clear by the numerous appearances of roving royal agents, the *qēpūtu ša šarri* discussed earlier, responsible for facilitating–but also, doubtless, for checking on–the activities of the local officials. (3) Provincial land transactions, like those around the capital, were not immune from royal involvement.[133] Finally, (4) the goods and individuals imported into the capital from the provinces and elsewhere are treated in the extant texts first as royal taxes, to be supervised by royal personnel, not as transactions along particular family lines. The point is underscored by two quota lists of workers, a number of them captives, given to three important persons we have met before, the brothers Qibi-Aššur, Ištar-ēriš, and Ubru–which assignment, however, is overseen by royal agents (*qēpūtu*) in Assur.[134] Of course, we must not forget the probability that individual provincial officials, like the Aššur-kašid family in Šibaniba, engaged in private commerce alongside, if not mixed up with, their official business. But this is not incompatible with an administration based on monarchical authority, all the more as there is no evidence of family commercial networks independent of the king and connecting capital and province on the

[130] Cf. Röllig, *Or.* NS 47 (1978), 426, 428-29. One could, of course, suppose that the name was given to a native Assyrian; but since it is a gentilic, "the one of Katmuḫḫu," it belongs better with one who was actually a native of Katmuḫḫu.

[131] The only other exceptions have already been mentioned: the official Urad-Šerūa, who may appear at Tell al-Rimah (see the last two references in n. 129); and the merchant Uballissu-Marduk, also probably to be found there (n. 116).

[132] See *KAJ* 113:21; 121:5.

[133] The one certain instance is TR. 3004:13′-14′ in Wiseman, *Iraq* 30 (1968), 179, which mentions the *ri-ik-si*/*ša šarri* (LUGAL). For the texts from the heartland, where royal involvement appears not infrequently, see Diakonoff (n. 49), 216-20; Garelli, *Sem.* 17 (1967), 6-12; and Postgate, *BSOAS* 34 (1971), 508-12, 514-17.

[134] See n. 127.

pattern, say, of the Old Assyrian colony period. In short, what we seem to have are local officials and their families using the opportunities afforded them to acquire private wealth—a phenomenon not unknown in other far-flung bureaucracies, and specifically attested also in Neo-Assyria,[135] when, it will be recalled, Postgate does agree that a royal civil service was in force.

The argument should by now be clear: While some connections can be supposed between the provincial officials and their families, and the great families of Assur, these are not of a character to affirm that the Assur families controlled the provincial government in oligarchic fashion. As Garelli has forcefully observed,[136] the monarchy was the real power. It chose the officials, whether from the Assur families or from other sources; and they all functioned, accordingly, as its subordinates.

F. Conclusion

The evidence we have been discussing, however sparse and uneven, shows by the mid-thirteenth century in Assyria a definite provincial system under royal control. Within this, territories or states less vital, because often too far from the Assyrian heartland, were left as vassals, obligated to regular tribute and state service. More important areas were converted to provinces, involving, frequently, population rearrangements and an apparatus of Assyrian supervisory personnel. Between these two categories, intermediate positions were eventually assigned, in a not unrelated way, to Ḫanigalbat and Babylonia.

To the clarification of this system, our five Amuda texts have made a small, but perceptible contribution. (1) They have enlarged the body of data from actual provincial sites, specifically that already known from the Ḫabur, revealing a new provincial seat for the thirteenth century, Ku/ilišḫinaš. (2) They have confirmed that the decisive period for the development of the provincial system was the thirteenth century. (3) They have also confirmed the character of the Assyrian provincial community as rather self-contained and separate from the native population. (4) They have illustrated the day-to-day operations of the provincial government especially in agriculture, and helped to explain the activities of one class of personnel, the *ḫurādu*. (5) And they have added to the examples of apparently private transactions alongside the official ones, reopening the question of extended wealthy families in the provinces and their relations with the great families of Assur.

It should be emphasized that our discussion has focused on the *nature* of this provincial system. To explain its origins and its rapid efflorescence in the thirteenth century would require more information than is presently known. It would also involve an examination of the underlying imperial ethos in Assyria, which is beyond our scope here. But two brief remarks on these larger issues may be offered, by way of conclusion. (1) Despite the presence of great families in both, this system stands at a considerable remove from that of the Old Assyrian colony period, when such families did, indeed, dominate the state, especially

[135] E.g., P. Garelli, *Annuaire de l'École pratique des hautes études IV. Section 110* (1977-78), 104-5, describing the official Bēl-issiịa.

[136] Garelli, *Sem.* 17 (1967), especially 20-1, where his comment is meant to apply to the entire workings of the Middle Assyrian state.

in international affairs, the monarchy exercising no all-encompassing authority.[137] Closer forerunners, perhaps, may be found in the more centralized monarchy of Šamši-Adad I and, as the use of *ḫalṣ/zuḫlu* suggests, in Mittanni, but too much remains obscure here to be sure.[138] (2) What is more certain is that our system is in clear continuity with subsequent Assyrian provincial practice, as we can follow it from the archive of Ninurta-tukultī-Aššur in the twelfth century through the Sargonid kings of the seventh.[139] Of course, this later practice became much more complex and extensive as the territorial base of the empire grew; and the complexity, in turn, was reflected in a vaster corpus of official and unofficial documentation. Yet in the essential elements–categorization and treatment of the conquered lands, character of the official hierarchy, and most important, the central position of the king–the later developments are all prefigured in the provincial system of the thirteenth century.[140] Provincial governance, thus, joins a number of other areas, cultural and political, in which the achievements of the thirteenth century represent a kind of watershed in Assyrian history.[141] Hopefully, future discoveries will clarify still other aspects of this crucial period.

IV. Postscriptum

When this study was already too far advanced, I received volume 3/1 of *Assur* (July, 1980), in which J.-M. Durand, M.-J. Aynard, and P. Amiet, building on the work of J. Nougayrol, present an edition of twelve new Middle Assyrian documents. All are now in the Musée du Louvre except for one (no. 12) owned by a private collector. Among these texts are two groups of immediate relevance to our investigation, since they are said to have been found at Assyrian provincial sites and to date from the thirteenth century. More specifically, they all fall into the period of Šalmaneser I and Tukultī-Ninurta I, thus confirming the evolution of Assyrian provincial policy discussed above.

The first of the groups comprises text 12, dated to a *līmu* of Šalmaneser I (l. 15) and

[137] Note the studies of M. T. Larsen, most comprehensively in *OACC*, 92ff., 109ff., 203, 209-11, 215-17, 218ff., 229-30, 368ff.

[138] Cf. Larsen, *OACC*, 219. On the monarchy of Šamši-Adad I, see the summary of J.-R. Kupper, *CAH*³ II/I, 2-6.

[139] On Ninurta-tukultī-Aššur, see Weidner, *AfO* 10 (1935-36), especially 14-15, 19-22, 24-7; and note the recent republication of the texts by Donbaz (n. 10). Neo-Assyrian provincial administration is treated in a number of studies. Besides the older, but still valuable ones of E. G. Klauber, *Assyrisches Beamtentum nach Briefen aus der Sargonidenzeit* (*LSS* 5/III, 1910) and E. Forrer, *Provinzeint.*, there are the recent surveys in Garelli and Nikiprowetzky (n. 35), 132-42, 275-81; J. Pečirková, *ArOr* 45 (1977), 211-28; Postgate, in *Power and Propaganda* (n. 92), 193-221; H. W. F. Saggs, *The Greatness That Was Babylon* (London: Sidgwick and Jackson, 1962), 238-60. Among more specialized investigations are those in nn. 63 and 93, as well as J. N. Postgate, *TCAE*.

[140] A full discussion of these continuities would require another paper. But it should be noted that they involve elements both of general strategy and of particular institutions. Among the former, one may mention the division of the empire into provinces and vassal states, with occasionally direct rule of Babylonia, and the practice of population arrangement. Among the latter are the ranks of *bēl pāḫete*, *šaknu*, *qēpu ša šarri*, *ḫurādu*, etc.–though the specific functions may not completely coincide–and the existence of private wealth among the provincial officialdom.

[141] For continuities in the treatment of the issue of Babylonia, see, e.g., Machinist, *CBQ* 38 (1976), 477.

alleged to come from Šūri (Durand *et al.*, 1), a formerly Ḫanigalbatian city in the Kašyari region (cf. Kessler, *Untersuchungen* [above n. 28], 57ff.). Although no discussion is provided of the actual findspot or circumstances of discovery, the provenience is suggested by the fact that the text records offerings to two temples, one explicitly said to be in Šūri (l. 12), the other so by implication (ll. 11-13). The former is identified as the temple of the city's tutelary goddess, the Hurrian Šūriḫa; the latter as the temple of IŠKUR, who is here probably the Hurrian Tešub; but significantly, in both cases the offerers appear to be Assyrians, to judge by their names (*mārat* Adad-bēl-gabbe; Adad-iddin??). What we have here, thus, is evidence of the attempt to accommodate local religious traditions in the wake of Šalmaneser I's consolidation of control over Ḫanigalbat.

The provenience of the second group of texts, nos. 6-11, is given as Tell Amuda (Durand *et al.*, 1-2); but whether all six really belong is not finally established by the editors. From the data they do furnish, a possible case can be made for nos. 8-11, in that 9-11, as they tell us (Durand *et al.*, 1), were reported by the dealer to have been found in Tell Amuda, while no. 8, for which no such report is noted, is at least connected to 9 and 11 by the fact that all three mention, as their only place name, the town (*ālu*) Kulišḫinaš. That leaves nos. 6 and 7. Here we have neither a dealer's report nor contextual connections to nos. 8-11 beyond a general date in the reign of Šalmaneser I. Strong uncertainty, therefore, about the membership of these two texts is in order; in fact, the editors intimate as much by talking at one point (Durand *et al.*, 45 *ad* l. 8) about "une unité de provenance" only for nos. 8-11.

Whatever number of texts we settle on, it is clear that the group brings us directly to the five Yale tablets published in the present study. The origin in Tell Amuda, the exclusive mention of the town Kulišḫinaš, and the fact that wherever the *līmu*s can be read (so in nos. 6, 8, 9, 10, 11) they date to Šalmaneser I and Tukultī-Ninurta I—all correlate precisely with our Yale texts, indicating that both groups come from the same (irregular) excavations in the mound of Amuda.

Unfortunately, no other specific ties between them can be observed, whether in onomasticon (excepting a possibly identical *līmu* in no. 6:22 and YBC 12863:7), seals, or content. But considered in their own right, the texts edited by Durand and his associates make several contributions to our knowledge of Assyrian provincial life in the thirteenth century B.C. No. 6, for example, if, indeed, it comes from Amuda, confirms the existence of a *rab ālāni* there, as well as of smaller *ālānu* lying around the town, as we had conjectured (above p. 20). It also appears to confirm the existence of land and seed grain under the control of the provincial administration, which in this instance have been lent out by the *rab ālāni* to an individual in an outlying *ālu* for farming, and are now being partly repaid. No. 9 involves another agricultural loan, here with repayment guaranteed by the property of someone other than the debtor. This arrangement, as Durand suggests (Durand *et al.*, 42), reflects the well-known Middle Assyrian institution of community (*ālu*) responsibility for the activities of its members, an institution bound up with the growth of extended families of wealth in the same period (see above pp. 29ff.), who not occasionally can be observed as owners or managers of such communities. And in nos. 8 and 11 we meet a type of document not noticed before in the Middle Assyrian corpus, the tax record, describing the "tax collector" (^{LÚ}*mākisu*) "inspecting and taxing" (*ētamar . . . imtikis*) a particular item belonging to an individual. Of course, the discovery of such records should come as no surprise, given the existence of inventories of taxes from the provincial and central administrations (above pp. 20-21) and the fact that the ^{LÚ}*mākisu* had been known in Assur texts

(Durand *et al.*, 45). Noteworthy is that on the basis of these two clear examples, Durand has been able to add three more, by a not implausible rereading of texts already published: *KAJ* 301 from Assur, and TR. 3019 and 3023 from the provincial site of Tell al-Rimah (Durand *et al.*, 45-46).

One final issue posed by the new Durand texts, or more precisely, by the treatment of them, needs discussion: the ancient name of Tell Amuda. In the English summary of their study (Durand *et al.*, 1), Durand and his associates suggest that it was Urkiš, contrary to the proposal of Kulišḫinaš advanced above (p. 4); but then they immediately backtrack in the direction of this proposal by observing: "the tablets, on the other hand, mention Kulišḫinaš in a privileged fashion." This confusion, unhappily, is not clarified by any further comment. Yet a solution may not be too far to seek. To begin with, it is indeed possible that Amuda was called Urkiš in the Old Babylonian and earlier periods and Urakka, a variant of Urkiš, in the Neo-Assyrian. The evidence is principally the Old Babylonian itinerary text published by A. Goetze, *JCS* 7 (1953), 51-72 and especially the report, vague and unverified though it may be, of W. J. van Liere, *AAS* 7 (1957), 91, that the two bronze lions associated with the Hurrian foundation tablet of Tišatal, king of Urkiš, were found at Tell Amuda (cf. B. Groneberg, *Die Orts- und Gewässernamen der altbabylonischen Zeit* [RGTC 3, 1980], 247; Kessler, *Untersuchungen* [above n. 28], 221-26). What is interesting here is that Urkiš/Urakka does not appear to be attested in the later second millennium B.C., specifically the Middle Assyrian period, thus in precise contrast to the name Kulišḫinaš, which is attested then, but not apparently before or after. The contrast is neatly expressed by the fact that in the Durand and Yale texts, which are Middle Assyrian and said to come from Tell Amuda, Kulišḫinas is the place of activity, never Urkiš. It may be proposed, therefore, that Urkiš/Urakka and Kulišḫinaš stand in complementary distribution, the latter replacing the former as the name of Amuda in the Middle Assyrian period. The reasons for this substitution remain unclear; but physically at least, they may have involved a shift of settlement to another part of the tell.

An incidental note may be added here. In the Durand texts, the four mentions of Kulišḫinaš are all spelled with *Ku-* (*Ku-li-iš/liš-ḫi-na-áš*: nos. 8:5, 12; 9:8; 11:8), not with the *Ki-* of YBC 12860:7. Given that both the Durand and Yale texts come from the same site and that the occurrences of Kulišḫinaš elsewhere are also all spelled with *Ku-* (see above p. 4), we may probably now judge the one instance of *Ki-* in the Yale tablet as a scribal mistake,  becoming  by a superfluous *Winkelhaken*.

V. Index of Personal Names in YBC Texts 12860 12864

All names attested in Saporetti, *OMA*, and Freydank-Saporetti, *Nuove* are unmarked. For the others:

+ = Names not attested directly in the above lists, but whose elements in other related combinations are found. E.g., for the unattested Amurru-salim, cf. the attested Adad-salim and Amurru-bani.

* = Names not attested directly nor in elements in related combinations.

• = Incompletely preserved names which cannot be compared to those in the above lists.

	Name	Reference
•	Abu-. . . .	12864:11
	Abattu	12862:8
	Adad-šāgime	12862:11 (see commentary *ad loc.*)
	Adad-šar-māti	12861:2
	Addi-(mu)šēzib	12860:20
	Aḫa-iddina	12861:3
	Aḫu-illika	12862:9, 18 (probably same person)
	Amurrīi̯a	12862:24
+	Amurru-salim	12861:7 (cf. e.g., Adad-salim and Amurru-bani)
	Aššur-šuma-uṣur	12862:20
	Ātanaḫ-Šamaš	12862:14
	Baḫu'u	12860:23
•	Bēl-šar[ru-/aḫ [(ḫ)u-]	12864:9
•	Da' 'ān-. . .	12864:8
*	Ḫasis?-Adad	12861:13 (cf. commentary *ad loc.*)
	Ibašši-ilī	12862:6
	Ibluṭu	12860:6, 9 (same person; see commentary *ad loc.*)
	Ištar-ēriš	12863:7 (*līmu*)
+	Ištar-le'at	12862:3 (cf. e.g., Adad-le'i and Ištar-rēmat)
	Kidin-Šamaš	12862:5
(+)	Mannu-iqīp	12862:22 (see commentary *ad loc.*)
•	Marduk-. . . .	12864:7
	Marduk-le'i	12861:9
	Mušēzib-Marduk	12860:3
	Nabû-bēla-uṣur	12860:26 (*līmu*)
•	Nergal?-. . . .	12862:12
	Putini	12861:5
	Qibi-Aššur	12861:16 (*līmu*)
	Rāši-ilī	12860:21
+	Rēmanni-ilī	12860:4 (e.g., Ilī-rēmanni and Rēmanni-Adad)
	Ṣilli-Amurru	12860:24
	Ṣillīi̯a	12862:17
	Ṣilli-Kūbe	12860:22
	Šamaš-aḫa-iddina	12862:21
	Šamaš-mušēli?	12862:2
	Šamaš-mušēzib	12860:5; 12861:11 (probably different persons)
*	Šarru-kī-ilīi̯a	12862:15 (see commentary *ad loc.*)
	Šubrû	12863:3 (see commentary *ad loc.*)
	Urdu	12862:20

PLATE I

YBC 12860

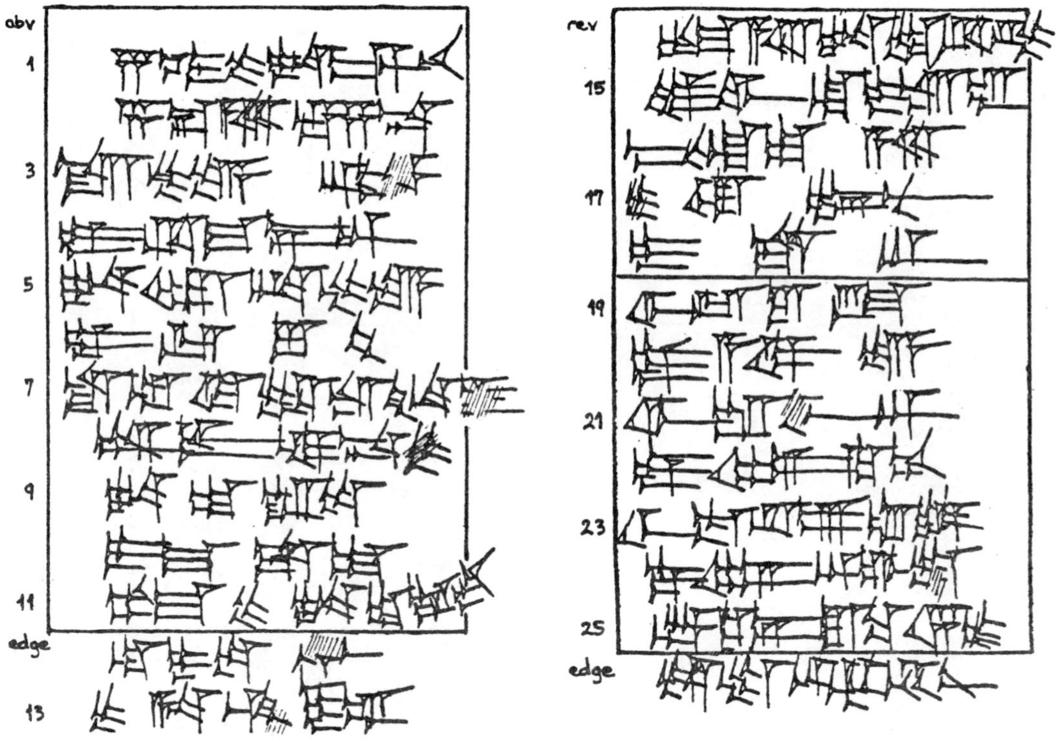

PLATE II

YBC 12861

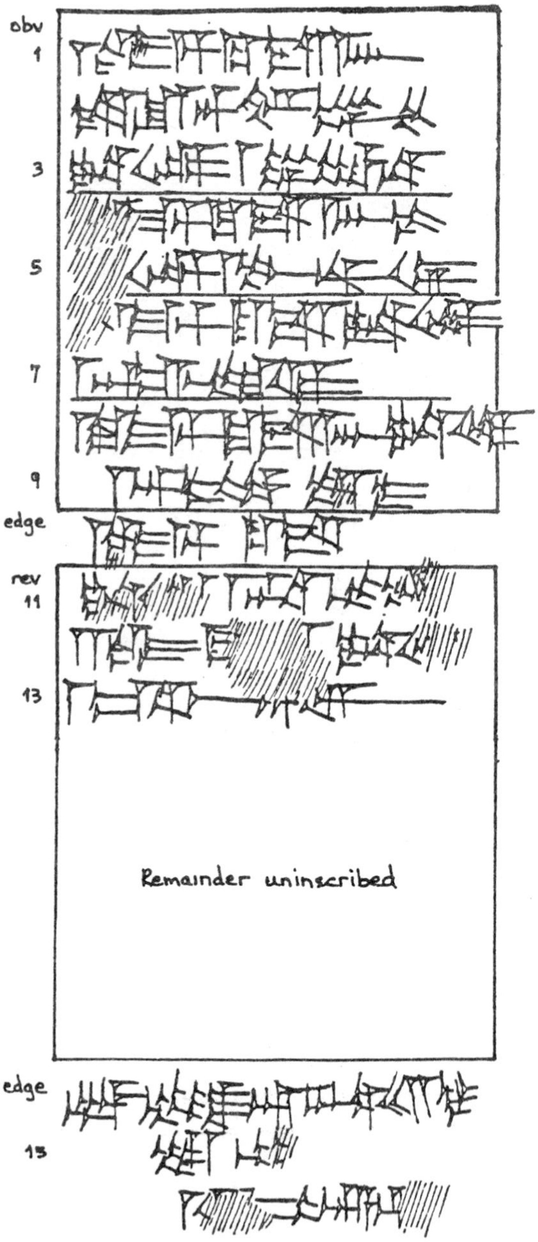

YBC 12862

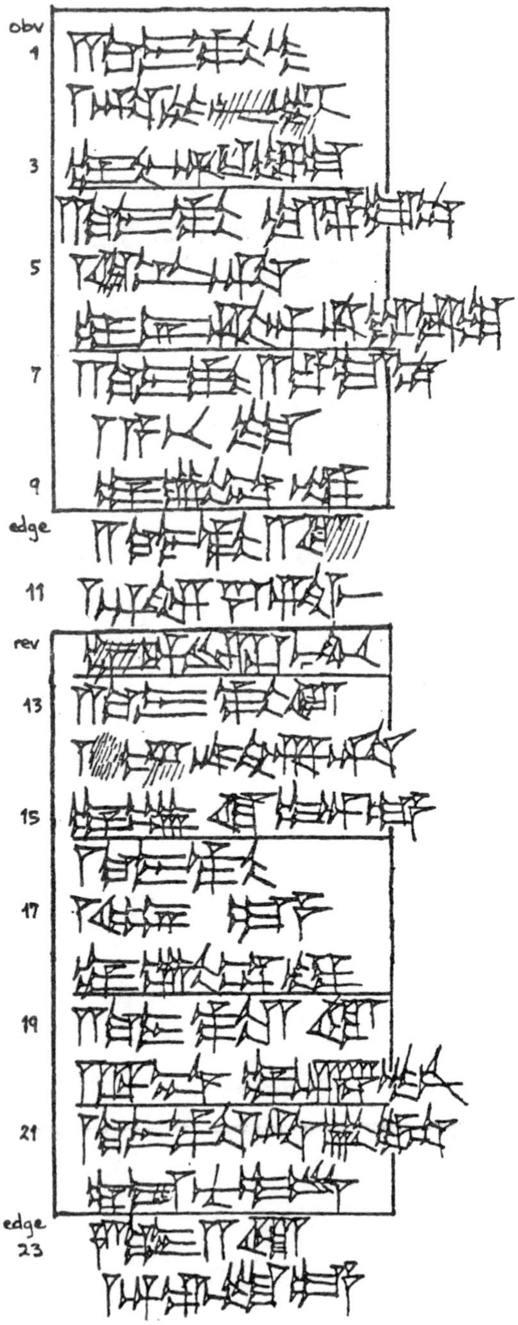

PLATE III

YBC 12863

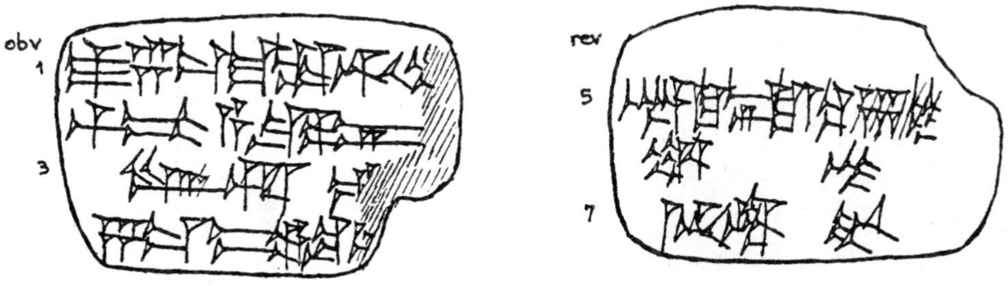

YBC 12864

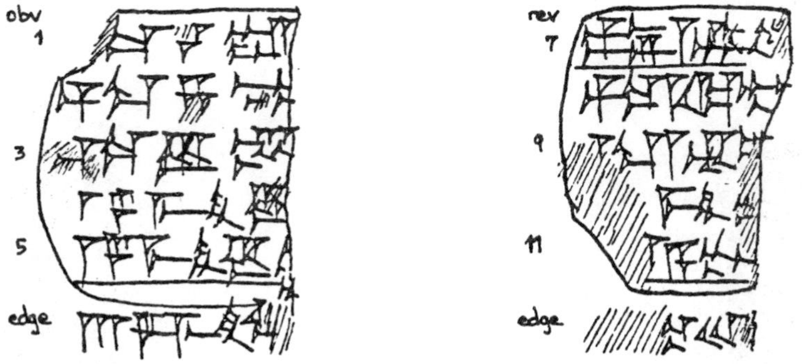

PLATE IV

YBC 12860
obverse

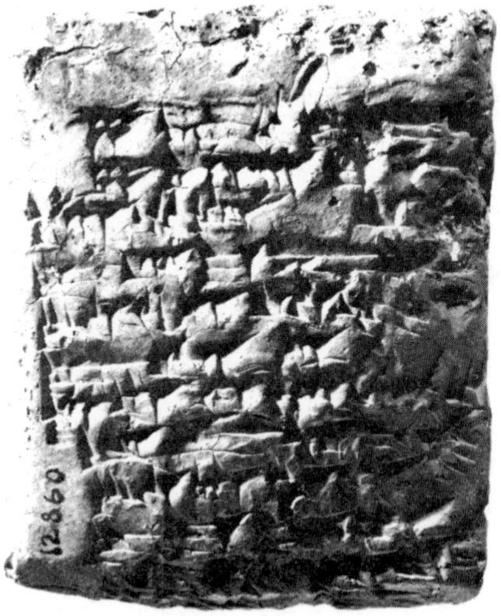

YBC 12860
left edge

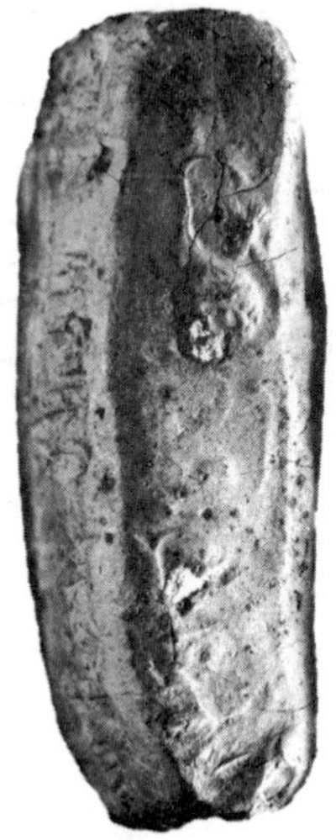

YBC 12861
right edge

YBC 12862
left edge

(All of above courtesy of Yale Babylonian Collection)

JNES STYLE SHEET
UNDENA PUBLICATIONS

General Procedures

A primary goal of Undena Publications is to publish at the lowest cost possible while keeping the highest possible standards. In order to do this we need your cooperation when submitting manuscripts. Please read the information below.

MANUSCRIPTS: Keep a duplicate copy of your submitted manuscript since this will not be included when proofs are sent to you.

PROOFS: Each author will receive proofs for corrections.

CORRECTIONS and CHANGES: Corrections and changes must be kept to an absolute minimum. Major changes, i.e. changes that affect more than a couple of lines, or a great many minor changes, will be at the author's expense, and subject to a $1.00 per change surcharge. All changes as submitted by the author on the proofs are suggestions only and may be disregarded at the discretion of the editor. Changes that affect entire pages will not be accepted.

COPIES: Besides 10 complimentary copies of the work, authors may take advantage of a one-time prepublication discount of 50% (plus postage and handling). Additional copies are available in unlimited quantity at 20% discount (plus postage and handling).

Manuscript Preparation

MANUSCRIPT: All material must be typed, double-spaced throughout on *non*-erasable and *non*-onionskin bond; photocopies are accepted. Isolated corrections may be entered by hand, but should be printed. The University of Chicago Press *Manual of Style* is recommended as a guide to style.

FOOTNOTES: All notes are to be typed, double-spaced, on separate pages with running numeration.

ABSTRACT: All manuscripts should be accompanied by an abstract of approximately 100-125 words.

TABLES and CHARTS: Tables and charts must be laid out as desired to appear in print, with explanations in the margin when the typed manuscript does not show clearly the intended format.

TITLES: Authors are strongly encouraged to divide their manuscripts into sections, subsections, etc., numbered and titled. There should be a table of contents (following the abstract) referring to these sections on the following model:

1. (Major heading)
    1.1. (Sub-heading)
    1.2. (Sub-heading)
        1.2.1. (Second level sub-heading)
        1.2.2. (Second level sub-heading)
2. (Major heading)

REFERENCES and BIBLIOGRAPHY: For all references please include (a) *Full* name of author(s), (b) place of publication *and* name of publisher, (c) page numbers of article.

UNDERSCORES:
Straight underline for *italics*: ______
Wavy underline for **bold face**: ~~~~~~
Wavy and straight underline for ***bold italics***: ______ ~~~~~~
Double underline for SMALL CAPS: ══════
Triple underline for REGULAR CAPS: ≡≡≡≡≡≡

SOURCES AND MONOGRAPHS ON THE ANCIENT NEAR EAST

Editors: Giorgio Buccellati, Marilyn Kelly-Buccellati

These two series make available original documents in English translation (Sources) and important studies by modern scholars (Monographs) as a contribution to the study of history, religion, literature, art and archaeology of the Ancient Near East. Inexpensive and flexible in format, they are meant to serve the specialist by bringing within easy reach basic publications often in updated versions, to provide imaginative educational outlets for undergraduate and graduate courses, and to reach the interested segments of the educated lay audience.

SOURCES FROM THE ANCIENT NEAR EAST

Volume One

Fasicle 1: R. I. Caplice, *The Akkadian Namburbi Texts: An Introduction.* 24 pp.

Fascicle 2: M. E. Cohen, *Balag-Compositions: Sumerian Lamentation Liturgies of the Second and First Millennium B.C.* 34 pp.

Fascicle 3: Luigi Cagni, *The Poem of Erra.* 62 pp.

Fascicle 4: Gary Beckman, *Hittite Birth Rituals: An Introduction.* 21 pp.

Fascicle 5: S. M. Burstein, *The* Babyloniaca *of Berossus.* 39 pp.

MONOGRAPHS ON THE ANCIENT NEAR EAST

Volume One

Fascicle 1: A. Falkenstein, *The Sumerian Temple City* (1954). Introduction and Translation by M. deJ. Ellis. 21 pp.

Fascicle 2: B. Landsberger, *Three Essays on the Sumerians* (1943-1945). Introduction and Translation by M. deJ. Ellis. 18 pp.

Fascicle 3: I. M. Diakonoff, *Structure of Society and State in Early Dynastic Sumer* (1959). Summary and Translation of selected passages by the author. Introduction by M. Desrochers. 16 pp.

Fascicle 4: B. Landsberger, *The Conceptual Autonomy of the Babylonian World* (1926). Translation by Th. Jacobsen, B. Foster and H. von Siebenthal. Introduction by Th. Jacobsen. 16 pp.

Fascicle 5: M. Liverani, *Three Amarna Essays* (1965-1972). Translation and Introduction by M. L. Jaffe. 34 pp.

Fascicle 6: P. Matthiae, *Ebla in the Period of the Amorite Dynasties* (1975). Translation and Introduction by M. L. Jaffe. 36 pp., 20 plates

Fascicle 7: G. Pettinato, *Old Canaanite Texts from Ebla* (1975). Translation and Introduction by M. L. Jaffe. 17 pp.

Volume Two

Fascicle 1: C. Saporetti, *The Status of Women in the Middle Assyrian Period.* Translation and Introduction by B. Boltze-Jordan. 20 pp.

Fascicle 2: N. Yoffee, *Explaining Trade in Ancient Western Asia.* 40 pp.